Editors
Dona Herweck Rice
Gisela Lee

Editorial Manager
Karen J. Goldfluss, M.S. Ed.

Editor in Chief
Sharon Coan, M.S. Ed.

Illustrator
Larry Bauer

Cover Artists
Chris Macabitas
Jeff Sutherland

Art Coordinator
Denice Adorno

Creative Director
Elayne Roberts

Imaging
Alfred Lau
Ralph Olmedo, Jr.

Product Manager
Phil Garcia

Publishers
Rachelle Cracchiolo, M.S. Ed.
Mary Dupuy Smith, M.S. Ed.

Practice and Learn

Fourth Grade

Compiled and Written by
Dona Herweck Rice

Teacher Created Materials, Inc.
6421 Industry Way
Westminster, CA 92683
www.teachercreated.com
©1999 Teacher Created Materials, Inc.
Made in U.S.A.

The classroom teacher may reproduce copies of materials in this book for classroom use only. The reproduction of any part for an entire school or school system is strictly prohibited. No part of this publication may be transmitted, stored, or recorded in any form without written permission from the publisher.

Table of Contents

Introduction

To Parents and Teachers

The wealth of knowledge a person gains throughout his or her lifetime is impossible to measure, and it will certainly vary from person to person. However, regardless of the scope of knowledge, the foundation for all learning remains a constant. All that we know and think throughout our lifetime is based upon fundamentals, and these fundamentals are the basic skills upon which all learning develops.

Within this book are hundreds of pages designed to teach and reinforce the skills that are mandatory for a successful completion of fourth-grade curricular standards. The table of contents (page 2) clearly delineates the skills. To use this resource effectively, simply refer to the contents list to find the work sheets that correspond to the desired skills.

Skills are reinforced in the following areas:

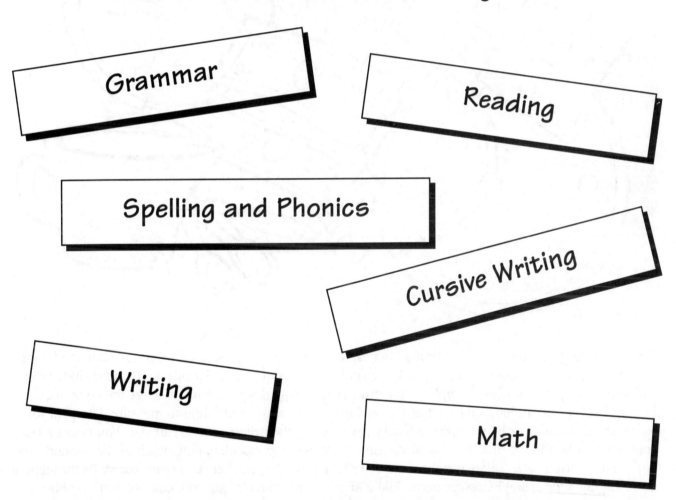

The work sheets within this book are ideal for use both at home and in the classroom. Research shows us that skill mastery comes with exposure and drill. To be internalized, concepts must be reviewed until they become second nature. Parents may certainly foster the classroom experience through exposing their children to the necessary skills whenever possible, and teachers will find that these pages perfectly complement their classroom needs.

Introduction (cont.)

In addition to this resource, there are a variety of hands-on materials that will prove vital when reinforcing basic skills. These include math flash cards; measuring spoons, cups, and weights; Celsius and Fahrenheit thermometers; a clock with hour, minute, and second hands; play money in various denominations; and a globe, maps, charts, and graphs. Kinesthetic learners will also benefit from plastic letters or numbers they can manipulate and use for figuring and writing, and every child will enjoy hands-on science experiences of all kinds.

Keep in mind that skills can be reinforced in nearly every situation, and such reinforcement need not be forced. As parents, consider your use of basic skills throughout your daily business, and include your children in the process. For example, while grocery shopping, let your child manage the coupons, finding the correct products and totaling the savings. Also, allow your child to measure detergent for the washing machine or help prepare a meal by measuring the necessary ingredients. You might even consider as a family the time you spend viewing television and calculate how much of the allotted time goes to advertisements. Likewise, there are countless ways that teachers can reinforce skills throughout a school day. For example, assign each child a number and when taking roll, call out math problems with those numbers as the answers. The children will answer "present" when they calculate the problems and realize that their numbers are the answers. You might also play the game of bingo with parts of speech, matching problems, or vocabulary words.

Since basic skills are utilized every day in untold ways, make the practice of them part of your children's or students' routines. Such work done now will benefit them in countless ways throughout their lives.

Nouns

A **noun** names a person, place, thing, or idea. Underline the words used as nouns in the following sentences.

1. The dog chased the cat up the tree.

2. Leaves fell from the trees as the wind blew.

3. My brother loves to play baseball.

4. I like to paint pictures with my new paints.

5. Freedom is something we celebrate in this country.

6. Love is very important in a family.

7. The electricity failed so we had no light.

8. The student wrote a story about a rabbit and a fox.

9. The soldiers came home from the foreign land.

10. The girl has been saving her money in her bank.

11. The boys will clean the desk when they finish the project.

12. Three monkeys swung from the vines in the jungle.

13. Her braid was tied with a pink ribbon.

14. Your soccer team has a better record than that team.

15. The museum was so crowded that we could not get near the exhibit.

By the Book

Choose a book. While reading, be aware of the nouns. Skim through your book to find the kinds of words described below. Look for a word that names . . .

1. a number _____

2. a color _____

3. a place _____

4. a girl's name _____

5. a boy's name _____

6. an animal _____

7. a sport or game _____

8. a flower or tree _____

9. a thing to eat _____

10. a thing to wear _____

Try some bonus questions! Look for a word naming something made of the following:

glass _____   metal _____

cloth_____   wood _____

Common and Proper Nouns

Proper nouns begin with capital letters, and **common nouns** are just regular nouns. The word *cat* is a common noun, but *Boots,* the cat's name, is a proper noun. Circle each word used as a common noun you find in the sentences below. Underline the proper nouns.

1. I live in the last house on Elm Street.

2. My dog, Max, and I went for a walk.

3. There are several Ryans in my class.

4. My family is planning a trip to the Grand Canyon.

5. "Mom, where is my shirt?" Jenny asked her mother.

6. Where is Primrose Park?

7. The only vegetable I like is broccoli.

8. Our cat is named Sylvester.

9. My teacher is Mrs. Simms.

10. Ricky, Sam, and Tim played football in the park.

11. Katie and Emily live in Jasper City, but their cousins live in Walton.

12. My brother and his friend liked the rollercoaster at the Maple County Fair.

13. March was too windy this year, but April was a beautiful month.

14. Brent and Kenneth played basketball last Saturday.

15. Have the children ever seen *Star Wars?*

Collective Nouns

Collective nouns are words used to describe a group of things. Below are some collective nouns used to group animals. Use the list below to complete the sentences. Notice that the word *of* plus a plural noun always follow the collective noun.

Example: People gather every year in March to watch the first *flight of swallows* return to San Juan Capistrano.

crash of rhinoceroses	tribe of monkeys
gang of elk	clowder of cats
pod of whales	school of fish
flight of swallows	murder of crows

1. A _____ snuggled under our porch during the storm.

2. A _____ were spotted in the meadow.

3. The fishermen were surprised to find a _____ close to the boat.

4. When we visited the zoo we observed a _____ .

5. A _____ were found near the corn in the farmer's meadow.

6. We saw a _____ when we visited Yellowstone National Park last summer.

7. We took the cruise from San Diego, hoping that we would see a

   _____ .

8. We saw a nature show on TV about a _____ .

Puzzle Change-O

Remember, a **noun** names a person, place, or thing. A **plural noun** names more than one person, place, or thing. To form the plural of most nouns, add an *s.* In the matching puzzle pieces, write the plural form for each word.

1. market	1.
2. pencil	2.
3. truck	3.
4. farmer	4.
5. cupcake	5.
6. student	6.
7. telephone	7.
8. computer	8.
9. picture	9.
10. penguin	10.

On the Go with Plurals

To form the plural of a noun ending with a consonant and a **y**, change the **y** to **i** and add *es*. Change these singular nouns to plural nouns by using this rule.

1. party _____

2. company _____

3. army _____

4. country _____

5. spy_____

6. puppy_____

7. liberty_____

8. fly_____

9. berry _____

10. factory _____

11. flurry _____

12. family_____

13. story _____

14. victory _____

15. baby_____

16. lady _____

17. monopoly_____

18. body_____

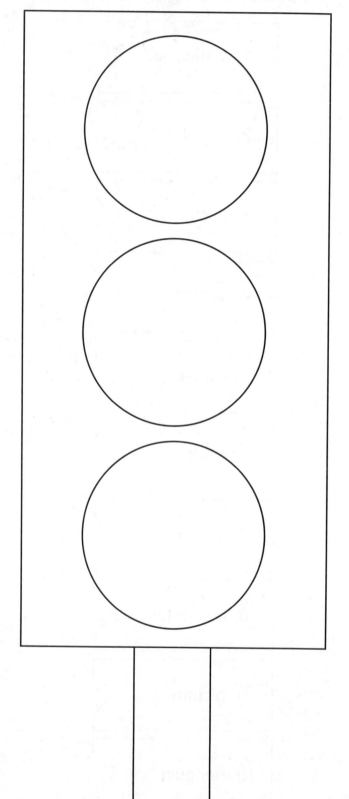

School of Fish

Nouns that end in **ch**, **sh**, **ss**, **x**, or **z** can be made plural by adding *es.* Color the fish below that use this rule. Write the plural form of each word.

1. 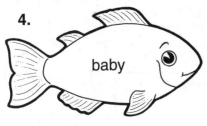 dish

_____

2. 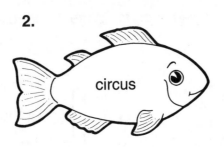 circus

_____

3.  party

_____

4. 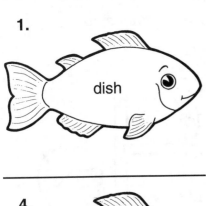 baby

_____

5.  buzz

_____

6. 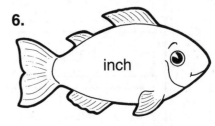 inch

_____

7.  key

_____

8.  pass

_____

9. 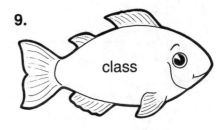 class

_____

10.  clown

_____

11.  coach

_____

12. 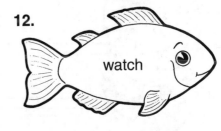 watch

_____

13. 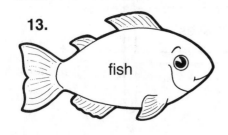 fish

_____

14. 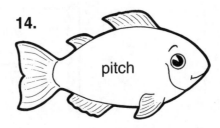 pitch

_____

15. 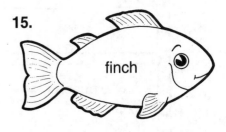 finch

_____

© *Teacher Created Materials, Inc.*

"Stepping Up" with Plurals

The first ladder is for singular words. The other ladder is for the plural form of each singular word. Climb each ladder by filling in the blanks with the matching singular or plural word.

Example: The plural for *pen* is *pens.* Write it on the second ladder step.

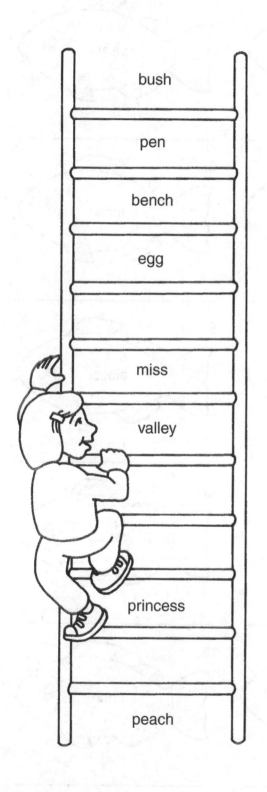
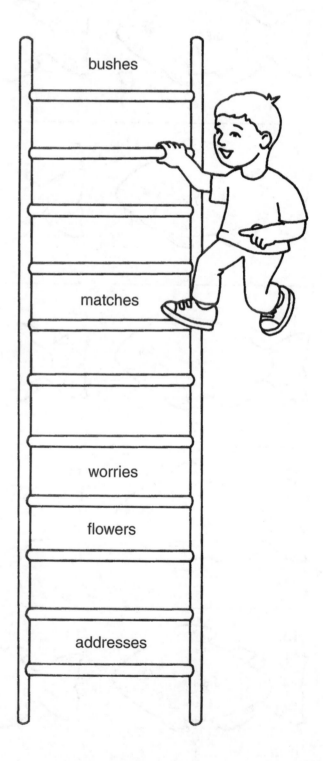

bush

pen

bench

egg

miss

valley

princess

peach

bushes

matches

worries

flowers

addresses

Predicting Plurals

Have fun predicting plurals. On each fortune cookie there is a noun. Write the plural form of the word on the fortune cookie. On the lines under the fortune cookies, write sentences using the plural words.

1.
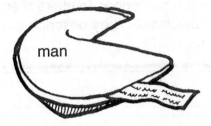

_____

_____

2.
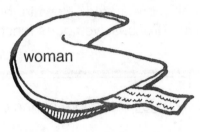

_____

_____

3.

_____

_____

4.
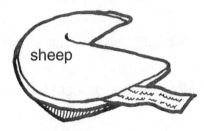

_____

_____

5.

_____

_____

6.
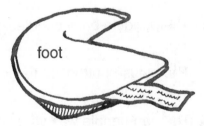

_____

_____

7.
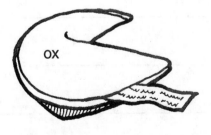

_____

_____

8.
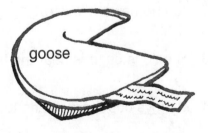

_____

_____

Possessives

Possessive nouns show who or what owns something. Singular possessive nouns are made by adding an apostrophe and then an *s*. Plural possessive nouns are formed by adding an apostrophe after the *s*. However, when a plural noun does not end with an *s*, an apostrophe and then an *s* are added. Rewrite the underlined nouns in the sentences to make them possessive. (Possessive nouns function in sentences as adjectives. They describe other nouns.)

1. The <u>doll</u> dress tore on the carriage. _____

2. <u>Lena</u> ball went over the fence. _____

3. Those <u>girls</u> jumping rope was tangled. _____

4. The <u>turtle</u> shell is like a home. _____

5. <u>Kate</u> mother brought her skates to the party. _____

6. The lost <u>child</u> father was relieved to find him. _____

7. The <u>boys</u> kites flew away. _____

8. The <u>penguin</u> baby cuddled against its mother. _____

9. The <u>blouse</u> button came loose. _____

10. The <u>pan</u> handle was very hot. _____

11. That <u>man</u> car is parked in the wrong place! _____

12. <u>Jen</u> homework is late. _____

13. The <u>lions</u> cage is near the tigers. _____

14. My <u>toys</u> cupboard needs to be cleaned. _____

15. The <u>play</u> cast was ready for opening night. _____

Action Verbs

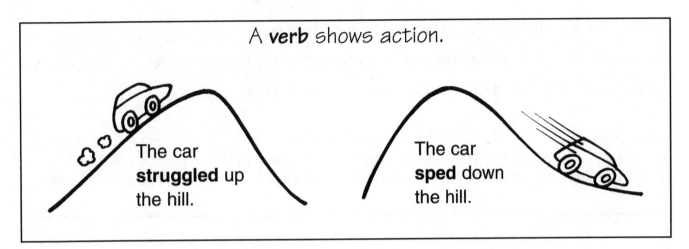

A **verb** shows action.

The car **struggled** up the hill.

The car **sped** down the hill.

Write the words used as verbs on the lines.

1. Barbara plays basketball well. _____

2. The bird flies over my head. _____

3. The bicycle makes Frank happy. _____

4. The children ran to the playground. _____

5. The balloon popped in front of me. _____

6. The pen ran out of ink. _____

7. I fell on the sidewalk. _____

8. I eat a piece of fruit each day. _____

9. The old horse stood quietly in the field. _____

10. Our teacher reads a story to us each day. _____

Take Action!

An **action verb** tells what the subject does. It shows action.

Examples: run, swing, jump, laugh, see, hit, leap

What are some of your favorite action verbs? Write them here: _____

_____

In the following paragraph, there are 50 action verbs. Can you find at least 40 of them?
When you find one, underline it in the paragraph and then write it on another sheet of paper.

In the morning, Benjamin woke up and jumped out of bed. He landed on
his brother, Timothy, who was asleep in the bottom bunk. Timothy sat up
and rubbed his eyes. He grumbled at Benjamin and then fell back on his
bed. Benjamin looked at Timothy for a long time. He wanted to see if
Timothy was asleep. Then Benjamin ran to the corner and grabbed his
horn. Benjamin blew into his horn and played some musical notes. He
liked the way his horn sounded. But he heard another sound. He
stopped and listened. A moaning sound came from Timothy. Benjamin
didn't like that sound. He grabbed his horn and ran out the door. He sat
on the front lawn and played some more music. The notes floated in the
air. He felt happy until he heard another sound. He stopped and
listened. A groaning sound came from his next door neighbor. Benjamin
ran into the backyard. He played his horn some more. He liked the notes.
Then he heard another sound. It was his mother. She called his name
again. He went inside. His mother took his horn and put it away. Then
she put Benjamin back in his bed. She told him it was too early to get
up. Benjamin's mother went back to bed, too. Benjamin tried to imagine
the sounds of his horn. Suddenly, he heard another sound. He stopped
and listened. Timothy snored again and again. Benjamin moaned. He
stuck his fingers in his ears, but he still heard Timothy. So he covered
his ears with his pillow. Soon he fell fast asleep.

We're Here to Help!

Some **non-action verbs** help action verbs do their work. They work together in a sentence, like a team. These non-action verbs are called **helping verbs**.

Example: People **can travel** in many ways.　　The non-action helping verb is *can*.

The action verb is *travel*.

The complete verb is *can travel*.

Find the helping and action verbs in sentences shown below. Use the following list of verbs to help you. Then fill in the chart at the bottom of the page by writing the helping and action verbs from the sentences.

Helping Verbs:	am	is	should	are	were	has	have	had	can	will
Action Verbs:	drink	ridden	pushed	driven	move	pulled	going	ride	seen	go

1. Jimmy should ride his bicycle.
2. An elephant is ridden in India.
3. The scooters were pushed by the children.
4. An airplane can move quickly.
5. Amy has driven a bus.

6. Sled dogs have pulled the children across the snow.
7. I have seen a bear.
8. You will go to a birthday party.
9. Henry is going to eat all the cake.
10. We will drink all the punch.

Helping Verbs

1. _____
2. _____
3. _____
4. _____
5. _____
6. _____
7. _____
8. _____
9. _____
10. _____

Action Verbs

1. _____
2. _____
3. _____
4. _____
5. _____
6. _____
7. _____
8. _____
9. _____
10. _____

Verb Tenses

The words below are written in the **present tense** (today). On the blank after each word, write its form in the **past tense** (before today). The first one has been done for you.

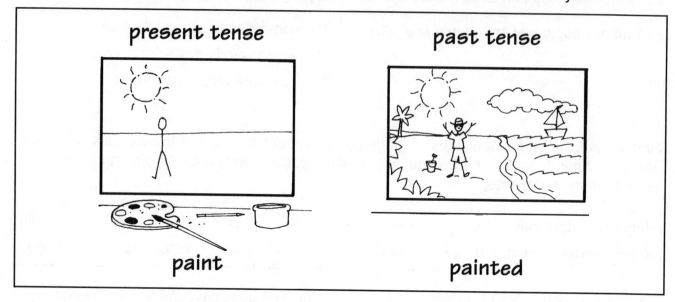

present tense	past tense
paint	painted

1. paint   __painted__

2. climb   _____

3. play   _____

4. laugh   _____

5. shout   _____

6. jump   _____

7. run   _____

8. see   _____

9. eat   _____

10. come   _____

11. make   _____

12. build   _____

13. sleep   _____

14. give   _____

15. take   _____

16. bring   _____

17. sing   _____

18. hold   _____

19. go   _____

20. write   _____

Past and Present

Verbs in the **present tense** show action that is happening now. In the **past tense**, verbs show action that already happened.

Change each of these present tense verbs to the past tense by adding *d* or *ed*.	Change each of the past tense verbs to the present tense by removing the *d* or *ed*.
1. turn _____	11. smiled _____
2. cook _____	12. folded _____
3. roll _____	13. closed _____
4. watch _____	14. painted _____
5. park _____	15. climbed _____
6. fill _____	16. shared _____
7. color _____	17. joked _____
8. fold _____	18. matched _____
9. close _____	19. laughed _____
10. look _____	20. played _____

Changing Irregular Verbs

Change the following irregular verbs from present to past tense.	Change the irregular verbs from past to present tense.
1. blow _____	11. caught _____
2. come _____	12. read _____
3. sing _____	13. rode _____
4. wear _____	14. drank _____
5. take _____	15. swung _____
6. cry _____	16. shone _____
7. make _____	17. paid _____
8. give _____	18. wrote _____
9. fall _____	19. swept _____
10. fly _____	20. tore _____

Was and Were

Write **was** or **were** in each sentence.

Four little birds **were** chirping a song.

1. What _____ that?

2. Where _____ you going?

3. I _____ at the movies.

4. We _____ cleaning the room.

5. She _____ very helpful today.

6. They _____ afraid of the big dog.

7. Jan and Laura _____ playing in the sand.

8. Tim _____ in the kitchen.

9. My friend and I _____ just about to leave.

10. Who _____ in charge of the show?

Is, Am, and Are

Write **is**, **am**, or **are** in each sentence.

Today **is** Marc's birthday.
How old **is** he?

1. Who _____ you waiting for?

2. Where _____ we going tomorrow?

3. I _____ very hungry.

4. The boy _____ a good reader.

5. The children _____ playing in the park.

6. We _____ having a good time.

7. They _____ having some trouble with their car.

8. Terry _____ a good friend.

9. How _____ I going to get there?

10. I _____ feeling very tired.

Just One or More?

Subjects and verbs are very important parts of a sentence. They need to get along well. If they do not agree with each other, your sentence will not sound right. It is important that they agree in number. A **singular subject** tells about one person, place, or thing. It needs a singular verb. A **plural subject** tells about more than one person, place, or thing. It needs a plural verb.

Examples

Singular Subjects		Plural Subjects	
dress	rabbit	dresses	rabbits
car	Michael	cars	Michael and Jason
boy	house	boys	houses
Singular Verbs		**Plural Verbs**	
has	jumps	have	jump
is	hops	are	hop
runs	sings	run	sing

In the following sentences, circle the correct verb. On the line before each number, write an **S** if you circled a singular verb or a **P** if you circled a plural verb.

_____ 1. The dress (has, have) a big bow in back.

_____ 2. These cars (runs, run) funny.

_____ 3. The boys (jumps, jump) from the tree.

_____ 4. The rabbit (hops, hop) around the yard.

_____ 5. Michael and Jason (sing, sings) this morning.

_____ 6. My house (are, is) yellow and white.

_____ 7. All the houses on our street (are, is) one story.

_____ 8. Michael (hop, hops) on one foot.

_____ 9. My old toy car (are, is) rusty.

_____ 10. Our rabbit (has, have) a large cage.

Now write your own sentences on the lines below. Write one sentence with a singular subject and verb and another sentence with a plural subject and verb. Make your sentences as interesting as you can.

1. Singular: _____

2. Plural: _____

Adjectives

Adjectives are words that describe people, places, and things. Circle the adjectives in the following sentences that are descriptive words.

1. The unusual man came to our front door.

2. A playful puppy ran through our yard.

3. I like the green bike with the long seat.

4. We can play with this funny, old toy.

5. I am wearing a new pair of gray shoes.

6. My mother is tall and pretty.

7. My teacher is smart and funny.

8. I saw a silly show on television.

9. The happy pig rolled in the mud in the large barnyard.

10. There was a small, black spider hanging from the shiny web.

11. The choir members wore colorful robes during their lively performance.

12. My grandfather is kind and generous.

13. Should I wear my orange shirt or my yellow one?

14. The little girls pretended to have tea at their imaginary party.

15. The night was quiet when the barn owl began to hoot.

Enchanted Enhancements

Sometimes a simple, complete sentence is all that is needed. However, at other times it is a good idea to give more details.

Descriptive language and additional information about the subject are very useful and make the sentence more interesting.

A word that helps describe something is an **adjective**. There are three types of adjectives.

- **Demonstrative Adjectives:** These point things out. They answer the question, "Which one(s)?"

    Examples: *this, that, these, those*
      I like this dress. Those cookies look delicious.

- **Common Adjectives:** These describe the subject in a general way. They answer the question, "What kind of?" or "How many?"

    Examples: *soft, warm, six, blue, sunny, tired, tall*
      The building is tall. The kitten is soft.

- **Proper Adjectives:** These are made from proper nouns and are always capitalized. They answer the question, "What kind of?"

    Examples: *Irish, Martian, African American, Native American*
      I love French cheese! There are many Japanese cars.

In the following sentences, circle the adjectives. Then, on the lines, write the questions (*What kind of? How many? Which one?*) that the adjectives answer.

1. I don't like this sandwich. _____

2. The old man came to the door. _____

3. Most French students speak English. _____

4. We're learning a Scottish dance tomorrow. _____

5. The yellow flowers are wilting. _____

6. I have three brothers. _____

7. For dinner tonight, they're serving a delicious, spinach casserole. _____

8. Give me your dollar, and I'll give you my comic book._____

9. Tim doesn't want that soft pear. _____

10. Watch out for the mean dog down the street. _____

11. My clueless brother threw away my homework._____

12. Those black shoes are too small._____

More Enhancements

Now it is your turn to enhance the sentences in the following story. Fill in the blanks with descriptive words or phrases. You may use demonstrative adjectives (such as *this, that, these,* and *those*), common adjectives (such as *birthday, large, frozen, lovely, three*), and proper adjectives (such as *British, German,* and *Jurassic*). You may also wish to use descriptive phrases (such as *weather-beaten* or *pocket-sized*). Have fun with this activity but remember to try for interesting images with descriptive language rather than choosing words or phrases that will make the sentences sound silly.

It was my _____ birthday so I ran home from school. When I got to my _____ house it looked like no one was home. "Hello!" I shouted. "Where is my _____ family? Your _____ son and brother is home now!" No one answered. I went to our _____ kitchen to see if there was a note. No note. Not even a _____ note. I went into the _____ room and turned on the _____ television. There was a _____ show on. I turned the television off. I went back into the kitchen to get something to eat. "I want something that's _____ to eat," I said to myself. I saw yogurt, but it was pineapple flavored. "I don't want _____ yogurt. I want _____ yogurt," I said, grabbing a _____ yogurt. I sat down to eat the _____ yogurt. Then I looked for something else. I found _____ candy. I was just about to eat it when the _____ telephone rang. "Hello?" It was my _____ mom. She told me she would be home soon but needed me to go into the _____ basement to get a _____ chicken from the _____ freezer. "Okay," I said. Then I ate some _____ candy.

The telephone rang again. "Honey," my mom said, "please get the _____ chicken from the basement now!"

"Okay!" I said again. As I walked toward the _____ basement stairs, I started wondering how she knew I hadn't gone down to the basement yet. I opened the _____ door. I slowly crept down the _____ steps into the _____ basement. I was getting the creeps. How did she know? Why was it so dark? The _____ stairs made creaking noises. Finally, I got to the bottom and waved my hand around to try to find the _____ light switch. I felt some _____ cobwebs and shrieked just a little. Just then, the _____ lights came on, and I heard _____ voices screaming, "Happy birthday!" I nearly ran all the way back up the _____ steps. My heart was pounding so hard I thought it would break right through my _____ chest! I saw the _____ basement was full of _____ people. They were holding _____ balloons and _____ gifts. Everyone I knew was there—my _____ mom, my _____ Aunt Amelia, my _____ sister Lindsay, all our _____ neighbors, and all of my _____ friends.

So _____ is where everyone was, and _____ was how my _____ mom knew I hadn't come downstairs yet. The _____ chicken, I just remembered! I went to the _____ freezer and opened the door to grab a _____ chicken. Everyone stared at me. Then they all started to laugh. "No, honey," my mom said, "we don't need a chicken after all. Tonight we're having _____ pizza and _____ birthday cake with _____ candles!" We went upstairs and had a party!

Articles: A and An

Articles are a kind of adjective. The three most common articles are *the*, *a*, and *an*. *A* is used before words that begin with a consonant sound while *an* is used before words that begin with a vowel sound. Write **a** or **an** in the blanks below.

1. _____crayon

2. _____ape

3. _____saucer

4. _____egg

5. _____monkey

6. _____pill

7. _____itch

8. _____orange

9. _____house

10. _____leaf

11. _____ ant crawled across the leaf.

12. Have you seen _____ purple butterfly?

13. I would like to eat _____ sandwich for lunch.

14. _____ apple a day keeps the doctor away.

15. _____ goat chewed on my pant leg!

Comparison Suffixes

Some adjectives end in *er* or *est*. These endings are used to show how people, places, or things compare to each other. The suffix **er** compares two nouns or pronouns and the ending **est** compares more than two nouns.

Examples: December is *cold.*   Mary is *young.*

January is *colder* than December.   Jane is *younger* than Mary.

February is the *coldest* month of the year.   Micheal is the *youngest* of the family.

Use adjectives that end in *er* or *est* to complete the following sentences.

1. Chris is tall, but Marcos is _____ than Chris. Carey is the

   _____ of the three boys.

2. Cookies are sweet, but cakes are _____ than cookies. Candy is the

   _____ of all three desserts.

3. An orange is small. A plum is _____ than an orange. A grape is the

   _____ fruit of them all.

4. Joe's room is messy, but Tom's room is _____. Of all the rooms in

   the house, the kitchen is the _____.

5. A rock is big. A hill is _____ than a rock. A mountain is

   the _____ of all.

6. A flower is pretty. A bouquet is _____. A garden is the

   _____ of them all.

7. Pearls are hard. Rubies are _____, but a diamond is the

   _____ gem of all.

8. This magazine is thick. That book is _____. The dictionary is the

   _____.

Adverbs

Adverbs are describing words that tell **when** (a time), **where** (a place), or **how** (how something is done).

The monkey eats his banana **quietly**.
(How)

Underline the adverbs. On the lines, write **how, where,** or **when** to show the way in which the adverb is used.

_____ 1. I walked quietly.

_____ 2. We will go tomorrow.

_____ 3. We can play later.

_____ 4. My cousins will come here.

_____ 5. The cheetah growled fiercely.

_____ 6. The mother sang softly.

_____ 7. The ballerina dances gracefully.

_____ 8. Yesterday I played baseball.

_____ 9. The orchestra played well.

_____ 10. He completed his homework quickly.

Ly Endings

Adverbs are words that describe verbs. Remember, **verbs** are words that show action. Many adverbs that describe an action end in *ly*. Make a list of 10 verbs. Then list an adverb with an *ly* ending that describes how the verb can be performed.

Example: The rabbit *runs* **quickly**.   *Runs* is a verb.

                                    Quickly is an adverb that describes how someone might run.

Verb	Adverb
1.	
2.	
3.	
4.	
5.	
6.	
7.	
8.	
9.	
10.	

Descriptive Occupations

Many adverbs end in *ly.* Look at the occupation statements below. Choose an adverb that fits each statement.

Example: "I work *painlessly*," said the dentist.

1. "I work _____," said the banker.

2. "I work _____," said the sea captain.

3. "I work _____," said the butcher.

4. "I work _____," said the hairdresser.

5. "I work _____," said the lawyer.

6. "I work _____," said the doctor.

7. "I work _____," said the teacher.

8. "I work _____," said the firefighter.

9. "I work _____," said the librarian.

10. "I work _____," said the astronaut.

Pronouns

Pronouns are words that are used in place of nouns. Some pronouns are *I, we, you, it, he, she,* and *them*. There are other pronouns as well. Read the sentences below. Rewrite the sentences using the correct pronoun to replace the noun in bold print.

1. **The boy** played baseball. _____

2. **The girl** swam across the pool. _____

3. **The children** climbed the trees. _____

4. **Mary and Frank** rode their bikes to school. _____

5. The team surprised **Lily** with a trophy. _____

6. Kim saw **the dog** run across the street. _____

7. **Mom** read the new best seller. _____

8. **Gary** saw a strange shadow. _____

9. The girls walked to **Mary's** house. _____

10. The family found **kittens** in a basket on their porch. _____

11. Where should I put **the presents**? _____

12. **My dad** put gas in the car. _____

13. **The players** won the championship!_____

14. Where is **the key**?_____

15. Please, give that to **Rick**. _____

Write About It

Use each of the pronouns below in a sentence.

1. it _____

2. he _____

3. she _____

4. you _____

5. me _____

6. I _____

7. we _____

8. they _____

9. them _____

10. her _____

11. him _____

12. us _____

Synonyms

When comparing and contrasting objects and ideas, it is helpful to use special words called synonyms. **Synonyms** are words that mean nearly the same thing. See the examples in the box below.

good, helpful	strong, powerful	gentle, mild
fast, quick	sour, tart	bad, evil
little, small	big, large	tired, sleepy

Circle the synonyms in each row.

1.	busy	tired	active	bad
2.	nibble	chew	hit	play
3.	cook	flavorful	tasty	show
4.	joyful	happy	sad	angry
5.	walk	fall	stand	trip
6.	pretty	huge	anxious	enormous
7.	worried	anxious	smart	angry
8.	mad	angry	funny	disappointed
9.	talk	kick	chat	sing
10.	laugh	sneeze	cry	weep

More Synonyms

Draw a line to connect synonym pairs.

1.	neat	see
2.	sad	calm
3.	thin	chilly
4.	look	skinny
5.	plain	powerful
6.	strong	stingy
7.	cold	large
8.	big	small
9.	cheap	wealthy
10.	quiet	pointed
11.	poor	simple
12.	little	unhappy
13.	sharp	spotless
14.	loud	needy
15.	rich	noisy

Synonyms and the Thesaurus

A **thesaurus** is a book that provides a list of words with the same, or nearly the same, meaning. Locate each word in a thesaurus. Draw a line to connect the synonyms.

1.	like	true
2.	snip	fat
3.	plump	infant
4.	fly	soar
5.	bark	similar
6.	clown	whole
7.	huge	cut
8.	real	gigantic
9.	entire	yelp
10.	baby	jester

Antonyms

When comparing and contrasting objects and ideas, another kind of word that is helpful to use is called an antonym. **Antonyms** are words that have opposite meanings. See the examples in the box below.

night, day	up, down	bad, good
sad, happy	fresh, spoiled	clean, dirty
dark, bright	cool, warm	large, small

Circle the antonyms in each row.

1.	laugh	smile	cry	run
2.	even	fast	slow	easy
3.	hurt	heal	harmful	sad
4.	shiny	sea	dull	air
5.	wake	sleep	rest	cat
6.	girl	bird	boy	enormous
7.	coffee	fire	water	tea
8.	truth	confess	fly	lie
9.	smart	lively	ugly	pretty
10.	furry	hard	light	soft

Find the Antonyms

Complete each sentence with an antonym. You may choose to use a dictionary or a thesaurus to help you find the best antonym. There are many correct answers.

1. A flower is soft, but a rock is _____.

2. Sugar is sweet, but a lemon is _____.

3. Fire is hot, but ice is _____.

4. Let's do the work now and not wait until _____.

5. Tell the truth. Don't _____.

6. Try to be kind and not _____.

7. The water is clear and not at all _____.

8. The sun rises in the east and sets in the _____.

© *Teacher Created Materials, Inc.*

Draw the Antonyms

Antonyms are words that have opposite meanings.

Draw two pictures to illustrate each antonym pair.

wet, dry	day, night
happy, sad	few, many
big, little	cry, laugh

I Spy Homophones

Homonyms are words that sound alike
but are spelled differently.
Use the clues below to supply
the missing homophone pairs.

Example: *Hare* and *hair* are homophones.

You can use them to solve the first
problem.

1. a rabbit and something on your head

    _____   _____

2. belongs to us and a measurement of time

    _____   _____

3. used to make bread and a female deer

    _____   _____

4. opposite of yes and to understand

    _____   _____

5. past tense of read and a color

    _____   _____

6. a story and the end of a dog

    _____   _____

Which Word?

Words that sound or sometimes look similar often have meanings that are not alike at all. Decide which of the two word choices on the right is the correct one to correspond with the word or phrase on the left and then circle it.

1. strength	mite/might
2. in no way	not/knot
3. well liked	popular/poplar
4. fruit	plumb/plum
5. without covering	bare/bear
6. cry	ball/bawl
7. forbidden	band/banned
8. French money	frank/franc
9. musical instrument	symbol/cymbal
10. cold	chilly/chili
11. odor	scent/sent
12. religious song	hymn/him
13. market	bazaar/bizarre
14. color	blew/blue
15. breakfast food	cereal/serial

Tune In to Homophones

Written on each television screen is a message. The messages are full of misused homophones. Rewrite the messages and correct the homophones.

1.

Whether Flash...heavy reigns dew inn an our.

_____

_____

2.

Next on The Whirled Turns...Elizabeth is never scene again.

_____

_____

3.

News Extra! A wild hoarse and dear escape from zoo.

_____

_____

4.

Watch Mussel Man weakly lift waits on Channel too.

_____

_____

5.

Special Announcement! Ice skating pear wins gold metals!

_____

_____

6.

Try a knew serial just for kids! Awesome Oats!

_____

_____

Synonym and Antonym Review

Synonyms are words that have the same or almost the same meanings.

Antonyms are words that have the opposite meanings.

Read the words below. Write **S** next to the synonyms and **A** next to the antonyms.

1. heat, warmth		11. quiet, loud	
2. litter, trash		12. buy, sell	
3. happy, sad		13. angry, mad	
4. speak, talk		14. bright, shiny	
5. hot, cold		15. long, short	
6. hard, soft		16. dark, light	
7. fast, slow		17. mild, gentle	
8. wet, damp		18. loss, gain	
9. loud, noisy		19. remember, forget	
10. hungry, starving		20. ignore, disregard	

Antonyms, Synonyms, and Homophones

List whether each pair of words is made of antonyms, synonyms, or homophones.

1. complex/simple _____

2. independence/liberty _____

3. dawn/sunset _____

4. colonel/kernel _____

5. empty/vacant _____

6. chute/shoot _____

7. board/bored _____

8. write/record _____

9. mix/separate _____

10. furnish/supply _____

11. fare/fair _____

12. plump/thin _____

13. over/under _____

14. job/work _____

15. air/heir _____

16. near/far _____

17. plain/fancy _____

18. beat/beet _____

19. move/transport _____

20. individual/group _____

Days, Months, and Holidays

What day of the week is today? _____

Did you use a capital letter to begin your answer? If you did, you used a capitalization rule.

What month of the year is today? _____

Did you use a capital letter to begin your answer? If you did, you used a capitalization rule again!

What is your favorite holiday? _____

Did you use a capital to start? If you did, you know the rules for capitalizing days, months, and holidays!

- Always capitalize the **days of the week.**
- Always capitalize the **months of the year.**
- Always capitalize the **names of holidays**.

That should be easy to remember. Now for some practice.

Put these words in order on the circle and capitalize them (start with Sunday).

- friday
- monday
- wednesday
- saturday
- sunday
- thursday
- tuesday

List the months of the year in order on the the lines. Don't forget to capitalize!

- january
- august
- february
- september
- march
- april
- october
- november
- may
- december
- june
- july

1. _____   7. _____

2. _____   8. _____

3. _____   9. _____

4. _____   10. _____

5. _____   11. _____

6. _____   12. _____

Capital Places

It's vacation time! Do you like to go to museums, zoos, or parks? Do you like to travel to lakes, oceans, rivers, or mountains? Proper names of places need capital letters because they are proper nouns.

Here is a list of places that need capital letters. Write the capital letters that are needed above the names of the places. Then choose three of the places you would like to visit.

pacific ocean	sahara desert	rocky Mountains
Grand canyon	North pole	hyde park
Mt. rushmore	san diego zoo	disneyland
amazon River	lake Louise	niagara falls

I would like to go to . . .

1. _____

2. _____

3. _____

In the space below, draw one of the places you chose.

Capitalizing Sentences

One of the most important capitalization rules is also one of the easiest to remember. **Always capitalize the first word of every sentence**. It doesn't matter whether the word is *I, you, me, Africa, a, the,* or *people,* the first word of every sentence is always capitalized. It doesn't matter whether it is a word that is normally capitalized or not.

Let's see how you do. In the story below, there are some words that need to be capitalized. Use a colored pencil or pen to write the capital letter above the letter that is there.

---

one day, Mike and Chris were riding their skateboards at the park. when they stopped to rest, they noticed something in the bushes. "what is that?" Chris asked. mike looked more closely. "it's furry!" Mike said. both boys stood and stared, and then they saw it move just a little bit.

"ohhh," Chris said, "that scared me!"

"it's a little bunny!" Mike exclaimed. sure enough, it was a scared little brown bunny hiding in the bushes. mike and chris cornered it, and then Mike scooped it up. he could feel its heart beating very rapidly.

the boys walked around the park asking people if they had lost a bunny. nobody claimed it, so Mike and Chris took it home.

mike sat in a chair watching TV and holding the bunny close to his chest. chris made telephone calls to try to find out who had lost the bunny. next, they made signs and put them up around the park and in the neighborhood. the signs said, "Lost Bunny" and gave their telephone number. no one claimed the bunny.

"you can't keep it," Chris and Mike's dad said.

"why not?" Chris asked.

"we already have a bunny cage," Mike added.

"well, okay," Dad said, "but you'll have to give it food and water every day."

the boys were happy. they named the rabbit "George," even though it was a girl rabbit. they fed her all the vegetable scraps from the kitchen, rabbit food, cabbage, dandelions, and water. george grew to be a big fat rabbit who would sometimes visit the neighbors' yards to eat weeds and dandelions which are, to this day, her favorite foods.

It's All Relative

In the following sentences, circle the letters that need to be changed to capitals and write the capital letters above. If there is a capitalized word that should not be capitalized, draw a line through the appropriate letter.

1. uncle Jorge sat on the front porch.

2. I said, "mom, what I really want to do is stay home!"

3. My mom and my dad won't be home until 7 P.M.

4. His grandma made a quilt for his birthday.

5. My Cousin and my Grandma will be coming with my mom.

6. Our Grandparents have a surprise for Aunt Aimee.

7. I wrote "Dear grandma," at the top of my stationery.

8. I wish my aunt lived closer to us; she looks just like mom.

9. Then dad stopped and looked behind him.

10. I like to go to grandmother Norton's house in the summer.

11. My favorite Cousin is Jimmy because he makes me laugh.

12. At the wedding we saw aunt Marsha and cousin Brad.

13. My Mom and Dad are taking me to dinner after the awards assembly.

14. At the reunion I saw Aunt Edith and uncle Jacques, and Cousins Kathy, Meredith, Hector, and Samantha.

15. For my birthday I'm inviting cousin Sarah, Cousin Leigh, aunt Susie, and my uncle, whose name is Mike.

Extension: Make a family chart on a large piece of butcher paper. Put your name and a picture of yourself (a photograph or a self-drawn portrait) in the proper position. If you have brothers and/or sisters, put their names (and pictures if you wish) next to yours. Your parents' names should appear above yours. Make as many lines as you need to represent your grandparents, aunts, uncles, and cousins. Be sure the lines appear in logical positions. A sample diagram appears below.

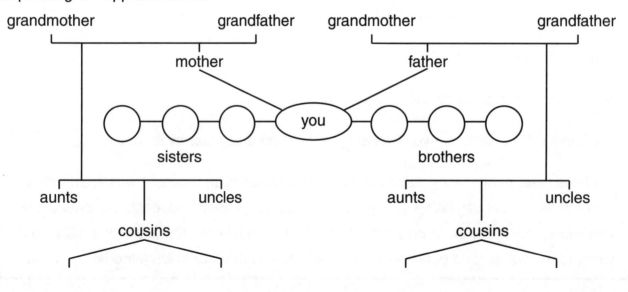

Con"trap"tions

Help the mouse get to the cheese before he gets trapped! Draw a line from the mouse hole to the correct contraction on the trap.

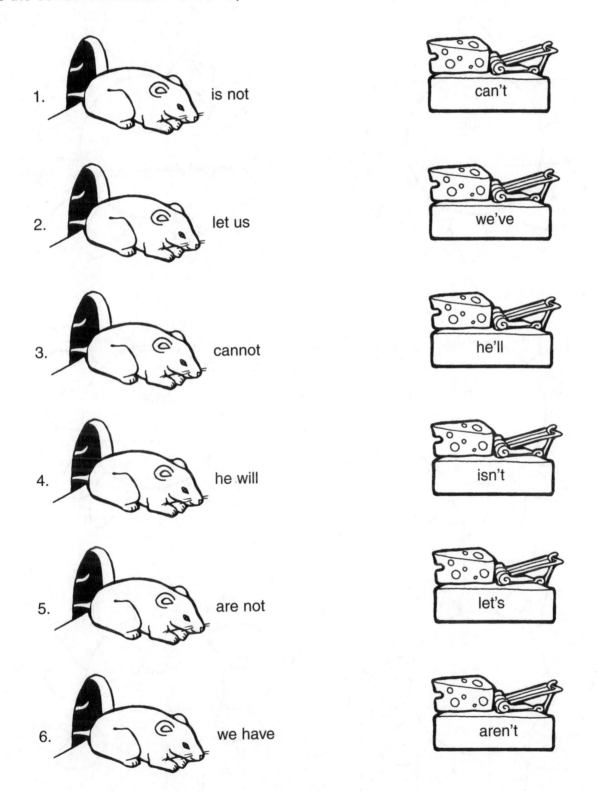

1. is not

2. let us

3. cannot

4. he will

5. are not

6. we have

can't

we've

he'll

isn't

let's

aren't

Blooming with Contractions

The contraction for *not* is *n't.* Write a contraction on each flower, using the word in the center plus the contraction for not.

Now You See Me; Now You Don't

Take out the apostrophe in the contractions and write the two words next to them that mean the same thing.

1. don't   _____   _____

2. wouldn't   _____   _____

3. won't   _____   _____

4. aren't   _____   _____

5. shouldn't   _____   _____

6. he's   _____   _____

7. I've   _____   _____

8. they've   _____   _____

9. we're   _____   _____

10. she's   _____   _____

11. you'll   _____   _____

12. didn't   _____   _____

13. isn't   _____   _____

14. wasn't   _____   _____

15. we'll   _____   _____

16. I'd   _____   _____

Contractions

Here is your opportunity to make contractions. In the story below, underline any words that may be combined into a contraction. On another paper list the contractions. There are 52.

I cannot believe it. I wrote 25 invitations that said: "You are invited to a surprise party for Serena. Do not tell her or she will not come." We could not have the party on any day but the 18th because it is close to Serena's birthday, and it is the only day in the entire month of April that is free. I stamped them and said to my dog, Sugar, "Let us mail these before it is too late." You will not believe what happened next.

It must have taken Sugar and me three hours just to mail the invitations after I had spent six hours making them because Sugar must have stopped at every tree. And then she barked at every bird; she would lie down if I tried to hurry her. Then she chased a cat up a tree, and she did not want to leave. There have been some new families who have moved in down the street, so Sugar wanted to sniff each of their new driveways. There must have been a dozen. A huge dog came running out at us. I should not have run, but I could not help it. It is instinctive to run when a snarling dog appears. It would have eaten us both alive, or at least that is what I was thinking when I decided that I had better run. I ran, dragging Sugar at the same time because she had decided that she would save the universe from the world's meanest dog. I will make a long story short by telling you that while I was trying to avoid death and while Sugar was trying to save the universe, the mean dog would have had us both for breakfast, but all three of us ended up tangled together in a whimpering, snarling knot of fur and tasty human skin. I was not doing a very good job of getting out of the mess, but at least the dogs were also stuck so we were not going anywhere. Then I heard a voice, "Who is this, Fluffy? It looks like we are meeting our neighbors." Fluffy? I was thinking it would have been better to name this dog Terminator. There I was. I was covered with dog slobber and fur, and I was not a pretty sight. Instead of meeting a new neighbor while standing, I could not believe that I was saying hello on my back while one dog, which should not be allowed on the street, was sitting on my stomach and drooling on my face, and another dog, which would not ever be allowed out of the house again, was licking my leg. What is wrong with this picture? My very good-looking neighbor must not have a very interesting life because he was laughing and enjoying the whole thing.

And if that were not enough, when I got home my mother told me that she would have stopped me if she had known that I was mailing the invitations. I had not been gone for three minutes when my sister called and told my mom that she had decided when to have her wedding and that she would like me to be a bridesmaid. Here is the part that convinces me that it is not a good idea to get out of bed on some days. She has decided to have her wedding on the 18th—you know, the day of Serena's surprise party? She has already reserved the church. I am so embarrassed. Now I will need to cancel the party. And my neighbor still laughs at me every time he sees me.

End Marks

Every sentence must end with a punctuation mark. A sentence may end with a period, a question mark, or an exclamation point.

- A period comes at the end of a sentence that tells something.

  Examples: I have a purple bicycle. Turn left at the corner.

- A question mark comes at the end of a sentence that asks a question.

  Examples: What color is your bicycle? Is that your house?

- An exclamation point comes at the end of a sentence that contains a strong feeling.

  Examples: Watch out for that car! What a wonderful surprise!

The following sentences need end marks. Think about which kind of end mark each sentence needs. Then write the correct punctuation mark at the end of each sentence.

1. I love my purple bicycle ☐

2. I saved enough money to buy it last year ☐

3. Would you like to try it ☐

4. My brother has a blue bicycle ☐

5. One time he crashed into me, and I fell off my bike ☐

6. Have you ever fallen off your bike ☐

7. Did you skin your knee ☐

8. I was so mad at my brother ☐

9. He told me he was sorry ☐

10. I'm so glad that my bike did not break ☐

11. Watch out for the glass in the road ☐

12. Don't ride your bike in the street ☐

13. Can you park a bike right here ☐

14. I have to go inside now ☐

15. Will I see you tomorrow ☐

Commas in a Series

Always use commas to separate words in a series. Place commas in the sentenes below to separate words in a series.

Example: James, Ralph, and Sara went to the park.

1. Tommy's three sisters are Amy Katy and Melissa.

2. Manual likes to play basketball baseball and volleyball.

3. Katy Melissa and Tommy do not play volleyball.

4. Amy wants to be a geologist an astronaut or a chemist.

5. Tommy, the youngest, has three dogs whose names are Skip Tiger and Rags.

6. Casey's favorite classes in school are math science and art.

7. Tommy Amy Katy and Melissa live in Dallas with their parents.

8. Tommy loves his parents his sisters and his dogs.

9. Manuel has three birds two cats and one dog.

10. Casey knows Tommy Amy and Manuel.

Names and Commas

Use a comma to set off a person's name when that person is being spoken to.

Example: Bobby, when is your book report due?

1. Mrs. Burnett may we go out to recess now?

2. Yes, we are going out to recess now Jason.

3. Mary will you swing with Tommy and me?

4. Sure Jason I love to swing.

5. Mary is going to swing with us Tommy.

6. No Jason I'm sliding with Matt.

7. Matt can swing with us Tommy.

8. Jason we can all swing first and then we can all slide.

9. Jason do you want to go on the slide first?

10. Tommy what time is recess over?

Set Off an Appositive

Always use commas to set off an appositive from the rest of the sentence.

Example: James, my best friend, lives a mile away.

Place the commas in the sentences below.

1. Amy Jones my best friend has a very large family.

2. Joe her oldest brother works for an airline company.

3. The youngest in the family Tony is only three years old.

4. The oldest daughters Karen and Sue often help with the younger children.

5. My other good friend Nicole and I spend a great deal of time at Amy's house.

6. Mrs. Jones Amy's mother says that two more children are coming tomorrow.

7. Amy's dad Mr. Jones works hard to take care of seven children.

8. Rags and Slick the Jones' pets get a great deal of attention.

Separate Day and Year

Use a comma to separate the day and the year from the rest of the sentence. Place a comma after the year when it comes in the middle of a sentence.

1. Jerry was born on October 5 1986.

2. My favorite Christmas was December 25 1992.

3. Susan's mom came home from the hospital on April 6 1994.

4. We took our summer vacation on July 21 1993.

5. My grandfather was born on August 11 1941.

6. On April 6 1994 Susan's mom brought a new baby girl home from the hospital.

7. My grandfather remembers July 20 1969 as an important date in history.

8. On July 21 1993 my family went to Hawaii for our summer vacation.

Separate Cities and States

Use a comma to separate a city from a state.

Example: Eric was born in Eugene, Oregon.

Place the commas in the sentences that follow.

1. The state capital is in Austin Texas.

2. My home is in Denver Colorado.

3. Her grandparents live in Bangor Maine.

4. Our tournament is in Ardmore Oklahoma.

5. Disney World is in Orlando Florida.

6. Her father is stationed in Fairbanks Alaska.

7. Queen Elizabeth lives in London England.

8. We rode the ferry in Seattle Washington.

Comma Review

Rewrite these dates and addresses using a comma correctly.

1. April 15 1972 _____

2. July 27 1640 _____

3. September 13 1910 _____

4. Monday January 31 _____

5. Sunday November 16 _____

6. Anaheim California _____

7. Albuquerque New Mexico _____

8. Quebec Canada _____

9. Bangor Maine _____

10. Little Rock Arkansas _____

Use a comma correctly in these letter parts.

11. Dear Joe _____

12. Your friend _____

13. Sincerely yours _____

14. Love _____

15. Yours truly _____

Add commas where they are needed in these sentences.

16. All birds have feathers wings and beaks.

17. The Shetland pony is small friendly and gentle.

18. A friendly playful dog makes a good pet.

19. I have three cats named Boots Muffin and Tiger.

20. I like to color with pencils markers and crayons.

Set It Off!

In the sentences below, add the missing commas to "set it off."

1. No Marlene does not like being squirted in the face.

2. Christopher how long have you been on the telephone?

3. Well just what did you have in mind?

4. Sure Laura I'd love another jelly donut.

5. My brother the world's scariest boy likes escargots.

6. The plane we are taking a 747 will have plenty of room.

7. You realize of course that you will not be allowed out of the house in that outfit.

8. My orthodontist Dr. Baugh decorated his office for Halloween.

9. All right if that's what you think, let's just eat all of the chocolate.

10. In the future we will be able to speak to our computers.

11. No kidding you went rock climbing?

12. We went to Bouquet Canyon a canyon near Valencia to attend a harvest festival.

13. You could read for example some books about the historical period in which your novel takes place.

14. For Valentine's Day my dad gave me two pounds of my favorite treat candy corn.

15. I don't care what you think I'm going to go back there and help that little boy.

That's Mine

When a word shows that something belongs to it, it shows ownership. *Possession* is another word for ownership. An apostrophe is used to show possession.

Example: *Friskie's leash* (To whom does the leash belong? The leash belongs to the dog, Friskie.) You usually add *'s* to a noun to show possession.

Show possession in the following examples. Don't forget the apostrophe. The first two have been completed for you.

1. food belonging to a cat   *cat's food*

2. a nest belonging to a bird   *bird's nest*

3. a bike belonging to Miguel   _____

4. a store that is owned by Kim   _____

5. a CD player belonging to David   _____

6. a book belonging to my sister   _____

7. a skateboard owned by my brother   _____

8. some toys that belong to a baby   _____

9. a desk that belongs to the teacher   _____

10. a brush that belongs to a painter   _____

Rewrite each sentence below, adding an apostrophe where one is needed to show possession.

11. Nicky ran screaming into Manuels house.

_____

12. My dad knocked down a hornets nest.

_____

13. I wish I could drive my brothers car.

_____

14. An alien ate Marielas homework.

_____

15. Grandpas spaghetti is the best in the world.

_____

Using Quotation Marks

Quotation marks and commas are used to set off quotations.

Example: She said, "I don't like bananas." (The comma after "she said" tells us to pause before speaking the quote. The quotation marks show exactly what was said.)

Place quotation marks and commas where they are needed in the sentences below.

---

1. Ryan asked What do you want to play, Martha?

2. Martha answered Let's play baseball.

3. Okay, we'll play baseball first said Ryan but let's play basketball after that.

4. Mom called The cookies are ready.

5. Oh, boy the boys yelled at the same time let's eat!

Write four sentences below. Make them a conversation between you and your best friend. Be sure to place the quotation marks and commas where they belong.

_____

_____

_____

_____

_____

_____

_____

_____

May I Quote You?

In the sentences below, place a check mark in front of those that need quotation marks added. On the line below each sentence, write the sentence again with the correct punctuation. If the sentence is correct, do nothing. The first one has been completed for you.

1. What is that bizarre thing upon your head? It looks like an octopus, said Mr. Grimmy.

   "What is that bizarre thing upon your head? It looks like an octopus," said Mr. Grimmy.

2. The teacher told the students to read the poem, "The Raven" by Friday.

   _____

3. I call my sister Idget, but I have no idea why.

   _____

4. "Hey!" Jacques shouted, "Didn't you hear the coach? He said, 'Stop when you get to the fence!' "

   _____

5. And then I will cover you with fragrant rose petals, Mama said, and sing a lullaby.

   _____

6. I found a book that said, Dinosaurs may be more closely related to birds than to lizards.

   _____

7. We have family nicknames, and my brother's is "Greasy Bear."

   _____

8. Did you hear what Nicole said? Amy asked us. She said, You guys are just too chicken to try it. She doesn't know what she is talking about!

   _____

9. I thought you would be too cool to go on the merry-go-round with me.

   _____

10. She watched *Somewhere in Time* so many times she wore out the tape.

    _____

11. My brother always talks in his sleep. Last night he said, "Hurry and purple it before the snails get it!"

    _____

12. After we watched *Twister*, we couldn't stop watching the clouds.

    _____

13. Come with us, Dad said, and we can stop for ice cream on the way.

    _____

14. I need to find the root word for transient.

    _____

15. Mom says we shouldn't say "Where's he at?" because it is not proper English.

    _____

Punctuation Challenge

Read the letter. There are 21 punctuation errors. Circle the punctuation that is wrong and correct it. Add any missing punctuation.

Dear Pen Pal

I love to go to the circus! On May 6 1999, the circus came to my hometown of Jackson Wyoming. A parade marched through our streets and soon the big top could be seen. Ken my brother, and I went to watch the performers prepare for opening night. We saw clowns, acrobats, and even the ringmaster. What a sight? Have you ever seen anything like it. You should go if you ever get the chance.

I also really enjoy playing baseball. My favorite team is the New York Yankees but I also like the St. Louis Cardinals. When I grow up I want to be a baseball pitcher, first baseman, or shortstop. Do you like baseball? What do you want to do when you grow up. I wish you could see my cool baseball card collection, but Kens collection is even better.

Oh, I almost forgot to tell you about my family! There are four people in my family. They are my mom my dad my brother and me. Scruffy my cat is also a family member. In August 2000 my grandpa will probably move in with us. I cant wait for that! Didn't you say your grandma lives with you. Ill bet you really like that.

Well thats all for now. Please write back to me soon. See you!

Your pal,

Brent

What Is a Subject?

All sentences have subjects. A **subject** tells who or what a sentence is about.

Example: Blake loves to paint. (Who loves to paint? **Blake** loves to paint.)
Blake is the subject of the sentence.

First, ask yourself who or what the sentence is about. Then, underline the subject of the sentence. Finally, write the subject of the sentence on the line. The first one is done for you.

1. <u>Blake</u> has a paintbox.

   Who has a paintbox? _____ Blake _____

2. The paintbox has three colors.

   What has three colors? _____

3. The colors are red, yellow, and blue.

   What are red, yellow, and blue? _____

4. Blake can make more colors.

   Who can make more colors? _____

5. Green is made by mixing together blue and yellow paints.

   What is made by mixing together blue and yellow paints? _____

6. Orange is made by mixing together yellow and red paints.

   What is made by mixing together yellow and red paints? _____

7. Blake loves to paint.

   Who loves to paint? _____

8. Blake's favorite color is blue.

   What is blue? _____

9. Mom hung up Blake's painting.

   Who hung up Blake's painting? _____

10. The painting is of a sailboat on the ocean.

    What is of a sailboat on the ocean? _____

Subject Practice

The **subject** is who or what the sentence is about. When an artist creates a painting of a vase full of colorful flowers set upon a white cloth in front of a blue background, the subject of the painting is the vase of colorful flowers. The rest of the painting just gives more information about the vase of flowers, such as where they are and what kind of light is shining on them.

Example: Swimming is fun. (What is fun? **Swimming** is fun.)
Swimming is the subject of the sentence.

First, ask yourself who or what the sentence is about. Then, underline the subject of the sentence. Finally, write the subject of the sentence on the line. The first one is done for you.

1. <u>Kids</u> love to swim at the pool and the beach.

   Who loves to swim at the pool and the beach? _____ **Kids** _____

2. Baseball is a fun sport to play or watch.

   What is a fun sport to play or watch?_____

3. Swimming is a good way to cool off when it is hot.

   What is a good way to cool off when it is hot?_____

4. I like to eat ice cream in the summer.

   Who likes to eat ice cream in the summer?_____

5. Summertime is my favorite time of the year.

   What is your favorite time of the year?_____

6. In the summer, Jeremy likes to take a vacation.

   Who likes to take a vacation in the summer? _____

7. Mosquitoes are numerous in the summer.

   What are numerous in the summer? _____

8. My skin itches when I get a sunburn.

   What itches when you get a sunburn?_____

9. Every summer seashells wash up on the shore.

   What washes up on the shore every summer? _____

10. The summer is over, but it will be back next year.

    What is over but will be back next year? _____

What Is a Predicate?

Just as all sentences have subjects, they also have predicates. The **predicate** tells us important things about the subject. It tells us what the subject does, has, or is.

Examples

- Tommy had a cold.

  What did Tommy have? Tommy **had a cold.**
  The predicate of the sentence is *had a cold.*

- Felicia jumps into the lake.

  What does Felicia do? Felicia **jumps into the lake.**
  The predicate of the sentence is *jumps into the lake.*

- The inner tube is leaking air.

  What is the inner tube doing? The inner tube **is leaking air.**
  The predicate of the sentence is *is leaking air.*

First, ask yourself what the subject does, has, or is. Then write the predicate of each sentence. The first one is done for you.

1. The water is very cold. _____ **is very cold** _____

2. We jump into the water. _____

3. Luke splashes us._____

4. Tonia is cold._____

5. She gets out of the water. _____

6. Nick does a handstand underwater._____

7. Everyone claps for him_____

8. The inner tube has a leak in it._____

9. Luke throws the inner tube onto the shore. _____

10. Tonia sits on the inner tube. _____

11. The inner tube deflates with Tonia on it. _____

12. Everyone laughs with Tonia._____

13. Tonia jumps into the water._____

14. Luke swims as fast as he can. _____

15. Tonia races Luke. _____

Complete Sentences

Before you can write a good story, you must be able to write good sentences. Remember, a sentence has a subject and a predicate. When the two parts are written together, all the words make sense. In each sentence found below, circle the complete subject and underline the complete predicate.

Example: (Mom and dad) took us to the beach.

1. Uncle Tony invited us to the baseball game.

2. His truck carried us to the field.

3. The parking lot was crowded.

4. We finally found our seats.

5. Uncle Tony bought popcorn and peanuts.

6. Two batters hit home runs.

7. Our team won the game.

8. People pushed to get out of the stadium.

9. We drove home late at night.

10. My sister was very tired.

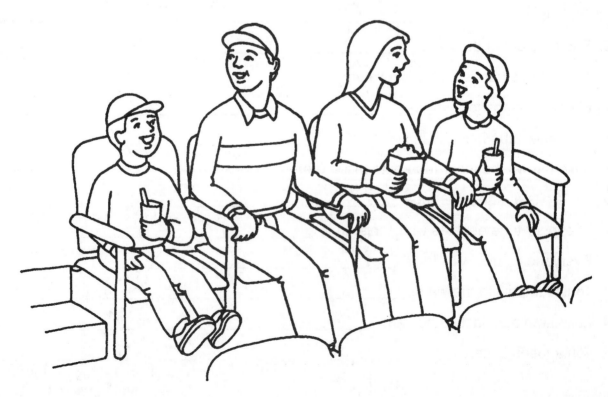

Take Your Pick

Look at the lists of subjects and predicates. Choose any five subjects and predicates and write five sentences. Remember to use a capital letter at the beginning of each sentence and punctuation at the end.

Subjects	Predicates
the oak tree	swayed in the breeze
a horse	jumped on a lily pad
a bullfrog	baked a birthday cake
I	walked down my street
my mother	wrote a letter
my friend	crashed the car
a giant	danced a jig
that snake	sang a song
my sister	jumped off the bridge
the clown	landed on my head
the parrot	skipped backwards
the monkey	played the piano
the teacher	blindfolded me
an organ grinder	skipped and whistled

1. _____

2. _____

3. _____

4. _____

5. _____

Word Muncher

A word muncher is a kind of monster that only eats parts of sentences. You can tell that a word muncher has been here because these sentences are full of holes. See if you can save these sentences by filling in the missing subjects or predicates.

1. The word muncher _____

_____

2. _____ (was, were) very hungry.

3. _____ jumped up and down on my bed.

4. Twelve gorillas _____

_____

5. _____ fell into the trunk of my neighbor's car.

6. A tiny little dancer _____

_____

7. _____ sat on a mushroom.

8. A large box of soap _____

_____

9. My Aunt Gertrude _____

_____

10. _____ (is, are) sloshing around in my pocket.

11. _____ (is, are) tumbling down the front steps.

12. My friend, Tiffany, _____

_____

13. _____ bit my ear!

14. _____ escaped from (his, her, their, its) cage.

15. Your elbow _____

_____

My Complements to This Sentence!

When you eat at a nice restaurant, the food tastes good because the chef does not cook just plain food. The chef makes the food with lots of extras, such as herbs and spices. If you tasted the plain food, you would say, "This is good." If you tasted the food with herbs and spices added, you would say, "This is delicious!"

The same is true with sentences. You can add information to a plain sentence to make it more interesting. As you have learned, every predicate has a verb. Sometimes a predicate has extra words that are called complements. A **complement** is a word or group of words that completes the predicate. It adds more information to a sentence.

Examples
• Jimmy jumps.
Jimmy jumps on me. The complement is *on me*.
• I walked.
I walked into the post. The complement is *into the post*.

Now it is your turn. Use your imagination to add some complements to the following phrases and sentences. Remember that a **complement** is a word or group of words that adds extra information to the predicate.

1. The race car driver sped _____

2. My sister screamed _____

3. The monster climbed _____

4. I saw a fat giraffe _____

5. An alien spacecraft landed_____

6. I want to run _____

7. Don't tell _____

8. My baby brother threw _____

9. A ton of broccoli fell _____

10. A big, purple bird flew _____

11. An ugly spider is crawling _____

12. Shameka and Patty ran _____

13. I don't want to see _____

14. The shooting star burst _____

15. Hector closed _____

More Complements

Sentence complements complete the predicate of a sentence. The complement can drastically change the meaning of a sentence. For each sentence below, write two different complements. An example has been done for you.

The car sped . . .
The car sped **around the racetrack.**
The car sped **through a red light.**

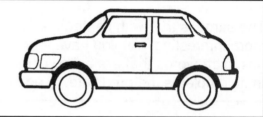

1. The parrot talked . . .

_____

_____

2. The girl wrote . . .

_____

_____

3. The people laughed . . .

_____

_____

4. The skaters raced . . .

_____

_____

5. The children danced . . .

_____

_____

6. My cat ran . . .

_____

_____

7. Their artwork hung . . .

_____

_____

8. The team of gymnasts demonstrated . . .

_____

_____

Sentence Emergencies

These sentences need your help. Be a sentence doctor and make these sentences better. Rewrite the sentences correctly. Put a capital letter at the beginning of each sentence. Use a period, question mark, or exclamation point at the end of each sentence.

1. tuesday is the day we go to the library

   _____

2. who is your teacher

   _____

3. the students in my class were reading

   _____

4. what a wonderful day it is

   _____

5. jordan, come play with us

   _____

6. watch out, Michelle

   _____

7. do you like math

   _____

8. i will paint today

   _____

9. what time is lunch

   _____

10. i got a sticker

   _____

More Sentence Emergencies

Unscramble these words to make a sentence. Remember to capitalize the first word in each sentence and to add punctuation at the end of each sentence.

1. bananas eat gorillas ripe

   _____

2. the door opened magician secret the

   _____

3. sense this makes sentence

   _____

4. broke the on egg my head

   _____

5. the nap a took dog tired

   _____

6. zookeeper bit the snake the

   _____

7. his pencil sharpened the boy

   _____

8. for computer the girl a her program made

   _____

9. mother called I phone my the on

   _____

10. the television watched Susie

   _____

Whoa!

You have learned that each sentence is a complete thought. What about sentences that do not stop when they should? A sentence that runs on to the next thought is called a **run-on sentence.**

> **Example:** Cake is the best dessert chocolate is my favorite flavor. (*run-on*)
> Cake is the best dessert. Chocolate is my favorite flavor.

Each of the following sentences is a run-on sentence. Write each run-on sentence as two separate sentences. The first one has been done for you.

1. My books are on the table my math book is on top.
   <u>My books are on the table. My math book is on top.</u>

2. They were closing the store it was time to go home.
   _____
   _____

3. Watch out for the slippery ice you could fall and hurt yourself.
   _____
   _____

4. I got a new blue dress the blue shoes match perfectly.
   _____
   _____

5. My brother made the team will I be able to play baseball some day?
   _____
   _____

6. I like to go camping the last time we went, we saw a bear.
   _____
   _____

7. My teacher was not at school we had a substitute.
   _____
   _____

8. I don't like lima beans I only want mashed potatoes.
   _____
   _____

9. Can you spend the night at my house we can have pizza for dinner.
   _____
   _____

10. My dog has fleas we had to get her some special medicine.
    _____
    _____

Bits and Pieces

You have learned that a sentence needs to be a complete thought to make sense. When a sentence is an incomplete thought, it is called a **sentence fragment**. Usually, a sentence fragment is missing a piece of information. You might not know the subject. The subject tells who or what the sentence is about. You might not know the predicate. The predicate tells what the subject has, does, or is.

Read the sentence fragments shown below. They are missing important pieces of information. Use your imagination to change these fragments into complete sentences. Rewrite the fragments as complete sentences, adding whatever information you wish. The first is done for you. Remember to capitalize and punctuate every sentence.

1. The big bad wolf
   The big bad wolf blew down the little pig's house.

2. went flying in the air

3. my best friend

4. Alan's birthday party

5. fell off the fence

6. was blowing big bubbles

7. a giant spider

8. ran into the street

9. her hamster

10. ate a bug

Fragment Search

On this page you will find five complete sentences and five sentence fragments. Write the five complete sentences using correct capitalization and punctuation. Use your own words to change the five sentence fragments into complete sentences. Be sure to write these new sentences using correct capitalization and punctuation. You should have written 10 complete sentences when you are finished.

1. bruce has many things in his room

   _____

2. books on shelves

   _____

3. is there a box of toys under the bed

   _____

4. a rug is in front of the closet

   _____

5. two stuffed animals

   _____

6. i can see trees from my window

   _____

7. the bedspread and curtains

   _____

8. my favorite game

   _____

9. look out for

   _____

10. latoya cleans her room every day

    _____

What's That You Say?

You already know about ending sentences with periods, question marks, and exclamation points. Sentences with these different endings have different names. Use the information below and on page 79 to learn about the four kinds of sentences.

- Sentences that make statements end with periods. They are called **declarative sentences.**

  Examples: Sunday is my grandma's birthday. It will rain tomorrow.

- Sentences that ask questions end with question marks. They are called **interrogative sentences.**

  Examples: Is this seat taken? Can I play? Do you want this? Where are you going?

- Sentences that express strong emotion end with exclamation points. These are called **exclamatory sentences**.

  Examples: We're going to Disney World! Tommy's cat won first prize at the fair!

- Sentences that make requests end with periods. Sentences that give commands or make strong or urgent requests end with exclamation points. All of these types of sentences are called **imperative sentences.**

  Examples: Put the book on the shelf. Watch out! Don't put those peas on your head!

- It might seem like an imperative sentence does not have a subject. You cannot see it in the sentence, but it is there. The subject is *you*. Test it for yourself. When someone says to you, "Please put the book on the shelf," the subject *you* is not in the sentence. However, you know that the person is speaking to you. The person could say, "You please put the book on the shelf." You can add the subject *you* to the beginning of any imperative sentence.

  Examples: (*You*) Wash the dishes. (*You*) Return the books.

Decide whether the following sentences are imperatives or declaratives. On the line before each number, write an **I** if it is an imperative sentence or a **D** if it is a declarative sentence.

_____ 1. The top fell off my new toy soldier.   _____ 6. I can't find my shoes.

_____ 2. Put me down, please.   _____ 7. Give me my hat.

_____ 3. Open your science books.   _____ 8. Marie, I will tickle you.

_____ 4. My dog ate my homework.   _____ 9. Stop!

_____ 5. Take out the trash now!   _____ 10. I warned you not to do that.

What's That You Say? (cont.)

Sentences that end with question marks are always interrogatives. **Interrogative sentences** ask questions. Another way to tell if a sentence is an interrogative is to ask yourself, "Does the main verb come before the subject?" If the main verb comes before the subject, it is an interrogative sentence.

Write five questions that you would like to ask your teacher.

1. _____

   _____

2. _____

   _____

3. _____

   _____

4. _____

   _____

5. _____

   _____

Great job! You have written five interrogative sentences.

Put a period at the end of each declarative sentence or imperative sentence that makes a request. Put an exclamation point at the end of each exclamatory sentence or imperative sentence that gives a command or makes a strong or urgent request.

1. I am very tired 🔲

2. Let's sit down here 🔲

3. What a wonderful idea 🔲

4. Ouch 🔲

5. Watch where you throw that ball 🔲

6. Well, then, let's have some lunch 🔲

7. The sandwich is for you 🔲

8. That lasagna is very hot 🔲

9. I didn't think you wanted lasagna 🔲

10. Sue would like a hamburger, please 🔲

11. Bob, you don't have to get so upset 🔲

12. This sandwich tastes good 🔲

13. I love roast beef 🔲

14. Take your brother to the park 🔲

Can You Handle This?

You have probably noticed that some sentences could be either exclamatory or declarative. The more writing you do, the more you will notice that you are in control. You, as the writer, determine whether or not sentences will express strong feelings. The way you punctuate affects the meaning as shown in the following examples.

Examples: 1. I got a B on the test!   2. I got a B on the test.

In the first sentence, the student is very happy and excited about earning a B. In the second sentence, the student is just telling someone that he or she earned a B.

Correct the paragraph shown below. You will need to remember everything that you have learned about complete sentences, capitalization, and punctuation. When you have finished correcting the paragraph, proofread it to avoid any careless errors. You may wish to change some of your answers. Revise the paragraph and read it one more time. After you have rechecked your answers, use another paper to write a new paragraph that includes as many declarative, interrogative, imperative, and exclamatory sentences as you can. This is your chance to be creative and use your imagination.

i went to the store because i needed to get something for lunch my

stomach was growling so much that a little boy sitting in a shopping cart

could hear it Mom, he said, he has a rumbly tumbly Shush said his

mother i turned to the little boy and asked i have a what A rumbly

tumbly he said and smiled shyly. A rumbly tumbly, a rumbly tumbly i

said over and over again the little boy started to giggle and i was even

hungrier than before yikes i said to the little boy. i have to get

something to eat before my rumbly tumbly tumbles the little boy stopped

giggling, pointed his finger at me, and said, go get something to eat

right now before your rumbly tumbly tumbles okay i said as i rushed

down the aisle toward the apples and bananas.

Consonants and Vowels

Most letters of the alphabet are consonants, but five of them are vowels. The vowels are *A*, *E*, *I*, *O*, and *U*. Every word must have at least one vowel. Sometimes, *Y* acts as the vowel in the word.

Look at the pictures. Do the items begin with a vowel or consonant sound? Write **V** for vowel and **C** for consonant and write what the picture is in each box.

1. _____

2. _____

3. _____

4. _____

5. _____

6. _____

7. _____

8. _____

Consonant Blends

List all the words you can think of that begin with the following consonant blends.

bl   **br**   **cl**   **cr**

dr   **fl**   **fr**   **gl**

gr   **pl**   **pr**   **sl**

sp   **st**   **str**   **tr**

Digraphs

When two consonants are placed together and form one consonant sound, they are called a **digraph**. *Ch, sh, th,* and *wh* are the most common digraphs. When you say them together, you only hear one sound. Digraphs can come at the beginning, middle, or end of a word.

Add one of the four digraphs to each letter group. Then say the words you have formed.

ch	sh	th	wh

1. _____ick

2. _____oose

3. _____op

4. _____ape

5. ma_____

6. _____ank

7. _____eese

8. _____eck

9. _____irst

10. _____istle

11. ba_____

12. wi_____

13. _____ip

14. ben_____

15. wa_____ing

16. tra_____

Long Vowel Quilt Square

Listen for the long vowel sound in each word. Color the spaces this way:

long a = red   **long e = purple**   **long i = yellow**

long o = green   **long u = blue**

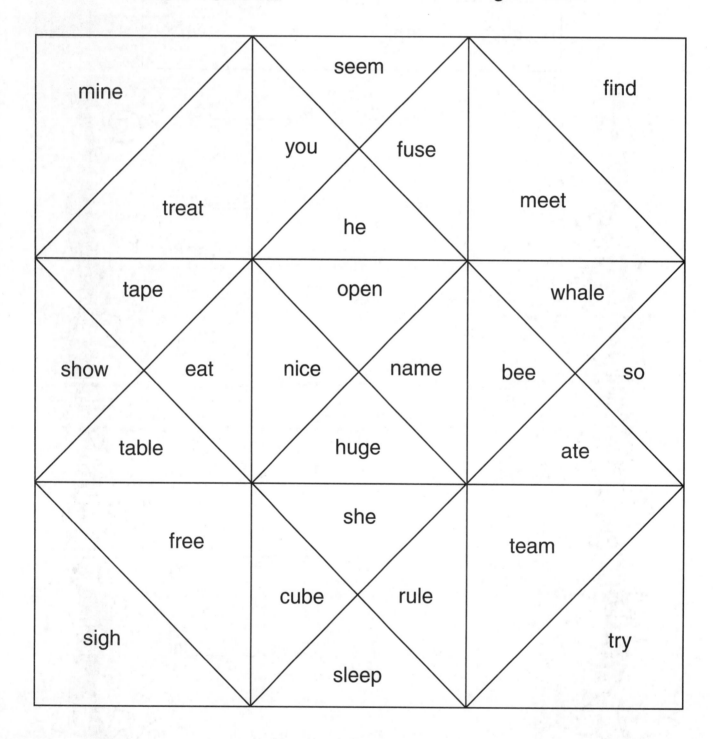

Short Vowel Quilt

Listen for the short vowel sound in each word. Color the spaces this way:

short a = purple   **short e = blue**

short i = red   **short o = yellow**

short u = green

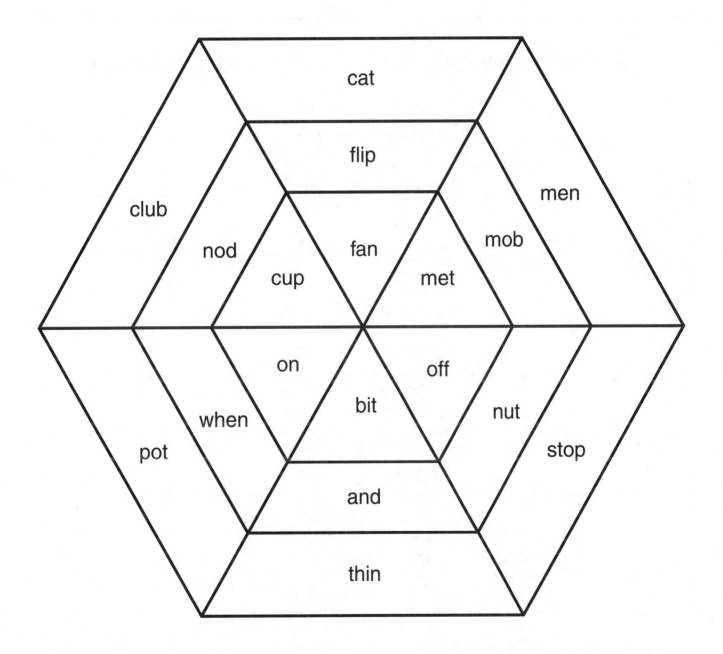

Long and Short

Read the words in the word box. If the vowel sound is long, write the word in column A. If the vowel sound is short, write the word in column B.

bat	bun	hot	maid	note
beach	cake	jack	moth	pump
beg	eat	let	mule	tin
boat	fish	light	muse	write

A (long vowels)   B (short vowels)

_____   _____

_____   _____

_____   _____

_____   _____

_____   _____

_____   _____

_____   _____

_____   _____

Silent E

Sometimes the letter *e* in a word has no sound, but its job is still important. It changes a short vowel sound to a long one. Read the words below. Then write the word on the blank and add an **e** to the end of each word. Read the new words.

1. can	2. sit	3. cap
4. tub		
5. dot		
6. not		
7. rat		
8. lob	9. bit	
10. cub		
11. grim		
12. fin		
13. bath	14. van	15. plan

1. _____

2. _____

3. _____

4. _____

5. _____

6. _____

7. _____

8. _____

9. _____

10. _____

11. _____

12. _____

13. _____

14. _____

15. _____

Silent Letters

Letters other than *e* may be silent in a word. Sometimes they change the sound of the other letters, and sometimes they do not. There are no easy rules for these silent letters. You must practice them to learn them.

Each word below is missing a silent letter. Choose a letter from the letter bank to complete the words. (Be sure to use a letter that will remain silent in the word.) Then say the words aloud.

b	h	k	t	w

1. _____rite

2. wi_____ch

3. _____hole

4. dum_____

5. _____not

6. no_____ch

7. _____new

8. com_____

9. _____onest

10. lam_____

11. g_____ost

12. w_____ale

13. _____rench

14. ba_____ch

15. w_____ip

16. _____our

17. ca_____ch

18. _____rong

19. _____rinkle

20. ma_____ch

21. _____night

22. _____nee

23. crum_____

24. _____nife

25. thum_____

26. _____nit

The Phunny Elefant?

The *f* sound is created in different ways. Sometimes the sound is made by the letter *f.* Other times it is made by *ff, ph,* or *gh.* Choose an **ff**, **ph**, **f**, or **gh** to complete each of the words below.

1. al_____abet

2. aw_____ul

3. cou_____

4. dol_____in

5. ele_____ant

6. el_____

7. enou_____

8. _____antastic

9. _____ish

10. _____un

11. gira_____e

12. lau_____

13. mu_____

14. _____onics

15. rou_____

16. ta_____y

17. tele_____one

18. tou_____

Gh

The letters *gh* are pronounced two ways. Sometimes they make the *f* sound as in *cough*. Other times, they are silent as in *sigh.*

Read the words. Write each word in the correct column.

cough	naughty	slough
daughter	night	taught
dough	right	though
enough	rough	tough
knight	sigh	trough
light	sight	

F Sound	Silent

The K Sound

The *k* sound can be made in four different ways: *c, k, ck,* and *ch.* Fill in the blanks with the correct letters to make the *k* sound. Read the words.

k	c	ck	ch

1. a_____e

2. ba_____

3. ban_____

4. bea_____

5. _____ane

6. _____ut

7. _____rumb

8. do_____

9. ja_____

10. _____eep

11. _____ey

12. _____ind

13. loo_____

14. ma_____e

15. ne_____

16. ni_____el

17. pa_____

18. po_____et

19. s_____are

20. s_____ool

21. s_____in

22. so_____

23. spo_____e

24. stoma_____

25. wal_____

26. ra_____e

Rhyme Z

Think of an animal that rhymes with each word. Write   on the lines.
Remember, rhyming words do not always end in the s

Example: *Chair* and *hare* rhyme but   e way.

1. big _____

2. sea _____

3. lake_____

4. drama_____

5. herd _____

6. habit _____

7. course _____

8. hear _____

9. box _____

10. log _____

Can you think of 4 pairs of rhyming animals? **Example:** *sow, cow*

1. _____   _____   2. _____   _____

3_____   _____   4. _____   _____

Rhymes

Rhyming words have the same end sounds, but those end sounds are not always spelled in the same way. Match the rhyming pairs by coloring each matching pair the same color.

1. alone	wrote
2. bowl	bale
3. coat	bees
4. home	fly
5. leak	frayed
6. maid	great
7. plate	known
8. seize	roam
9. sigh	roll
10. soap	rope
11. tail	taught
12. thought	week

Compound Words

A **compound** is combination of two or more words to create a new word. Write a word in the blank between each set of words. The trick is that the new word must complete a compound word both to the left and to the right of it. The first one has been done for you.

1. news   _____ **paper** _____   boy

2. drop   _____   side

3. frog   _____   hood

4. foot   _____   room

5. honey   _____   light

6. water   _____   out

7. head   _____   house

8. look   _____   side

9. time   _____   spoon

10. text   _____   case

11. left   _____   board

12. birth   _____   dream

13. dark   _____   mate

14. round   _____   keep

15. butter   _____   cake

More Compound Words

Choose a word from column **A** or **B** and combine it with a word from column **C** or **D** to make a compound word. Some words will go together in more than one combination, but there is only one combination that will use all of the words.

A	B
cup	handle
foot	jelly
gold	over
high	pony
pepper	rain
rail	silver
shoe	suit
spot	tip
sun	wind
sweat	wrist

C	D
ball	case
bar	fish
bow	fish
cake	light
lace	mill
look	mint
set	shirt
tail	toe
watch	ware
way	way

Hidden Compounds

A **compound word** is a single word that is made by joining two smaller words.

Examples: starlight, treetop, doorbell

How many compound words can you find in the picture? See if you can find 12.

Stressed Out Syllables

Words are divided into sounds called **syllables**. Two-syllable words have a stressed and unstressed syllable. A stressed syllable is the sound spoken loudest in a word. The unstressed syllable is the sound which is spoken more softly.

Rule #1

When a word has a double consonant, the word is divided between the two consonants.

Example: *bub´-ble*

Divide each word below into syllables and place a stressed syllable mark (´) on the syllable you think is stressed. Use a dictionary to check your answers.

1. pillow   _____

2. fellow   _____

3. pizza   _____

4. suppose   _____

5. surround   _____

6. scissors   _____

7. collect   _____

8. hurrah   _____

9. address   _____

10. silly   _____

Stressed Out Syllables (cont.)

Rule #2

When a word ends in a consonant plus *le*, the word is divided before the consonant.

Example: pur´-ple

Divide each word below into syllables and place a stressed syllable mark (´) on the syllable you think is stressed. Use a dictionary to check your answers.

1. turtle   _____

2. beetle   _____

3. bubble   _____

4. candle   _____

5. juggle   _____

6. hustle   _____

7. baffle   _____

8. cradle   _____

9. bottle   _____

10. trouble   _____

Stressed Out Syllables (cont.)

Rule #3

When the first vowel in a word has the short vowel sound, the word is divided after the next consonant.

Example: shad´-ow

Divide each word below into syllables, and place a stressed syllable mark (´) on the syllable you think is stressed. Use a dictionary to check your answers.

1. cartoon _____

2. cinder _____

3. droplet _____

4. extra _____

5. express _____

6. imprint _____

7. jungle _____

8. salad _____

9. magic _____

10. picture _____

Stressed Out Syllables (cont.)

Rule #4

When the first vowel in a word has the long vowel sound, the word is divided after that vowel.

Example: ba´-by

Divide each word below into syllables, and place a stressed syllable mark (´) on the syllable you think is stressed. Use a dictionary to check your answers.

1. humor   _____

2. able   _____

3. begin   _____

4. kiwi   _____

5. paper   _____

6. locate   _____

7. open   _____

8. profile   _____

9. rosette   _____

10. erupt   _____

Getting to the Root of It

Sometimes a word has letters added to the beginning or end of it that change the meaning of the word. The main word is called the **root word**, and the added letters are **prefixes** and **suffixes**. For example, in the word *soundless* the root word is *sound,* and in the word *unusual* the root word is *usual.* Notice how the meanings of these two words change with the added letters.

Read the words below. Write the root words in the spaces provided.

1. irresponsible _____

2. misunderstand _____

3. meaningful _____

4. worthless _____

5. immaterial _____

6. disengage _____

7. unaware _____

8. prearrange _____

9. semicircle _____

10. biweekly _____

11. mountainous _____

12. unicycle _____

13. triangle _____

14. nonsense _____

15. admiralty _____

Root It Out

On each flower is the name of a person who does an action. Find the root word in each name and write it below the flower. (**Note:** Sometimes letters from the root word are left off or changed to form the new word. Be sure to spell the root word correctly.)

1.

sailor

_____

2.

runner

_____

3.
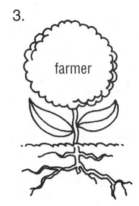
farmer

_____

4.

buyer

_____

5.
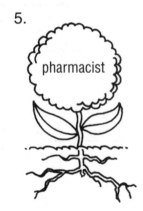
pharmacist

_____

6.
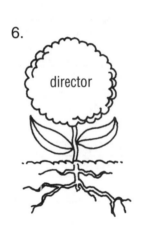
director

_____

7.

dancer

_____

8.
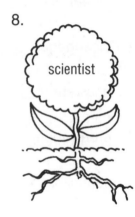
scientist

_____

9.

photographer

_____

10.
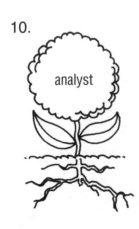
analyst

_____

11.
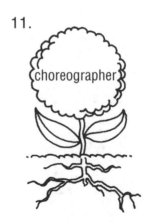
choreographer

_____

12.

biographer

_____

102

© *Teacher Created Materials, Inc.*

Break It Up

A **prefix** is one or more syllables at the beginning of a root word. When a word has a prefix, the syllable division is between the prefix and the root word. Circle the prefixes in the following cards. Write the word on the cards using hyphens to divide it into syllables.

unknown	**rephrase**
disrespect	**remake**
precook	**misalign**

Prepare for Prefixes

Here are nine common prefixes. How many words can you find that begin with these prefixes? Write them in the columns. One word in each column has been done for you.

un	dis	pre
unusual	discover	preorder

under	re	mis
understand	remake	mistake

ir	over	im
irresponsible	overwrought	immaterial

Painting with Prefixes

The prefix **un** can mean *not* or *opposite of*.

The prefix **re** can mean *again* or *back*.

Write the word on the paint can that tells the meaning of the clue.

Color the paint cans with the prefix *un* green.

Color the paint cans with the prefix *re* yellow.

1.

heat again

2.

playback

3.

not safe

4.

opposite of lucky

5.

do again

6.

not fair

7.

read again

8.

write again

9.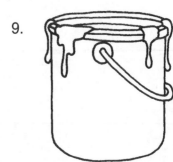

opposite of cover

Prefix Party

The prefix **over** can mean *too much*. The prefix **under** can mean *not enough*. Circle the words in the paragraph containing the prefixes *over* and *under*. Then write each word and its meaning on the lines below.

Kate was excited! She was going to have her birthday party with all her friends. That morning she overslept! She was behind on all her chores. She quickly overstuffed her toy box and underwatered the plants. She even forgot Shadow, her cat, and left her underfed. When she was washing the dishes, the water accidentally overflowed onto the floor. She was in such a rush! She took her birthday cake out of the oven too soon and then it was undercooked. She thought to herself, "I'm glad my birthday only comes once a year."

Word   **Meaning**

_____   _____

_____   _____

_____   _____

_____   _____

_____   _____

_____   _____

Surfing with Suffixes

A **suffix** is one or more syllables at the end of a root word. When a word has a suffix, the syllable division is between the suffix and the root word. Circle the suffix in each word and then rewrite each word on the waves with a hyphen to divide each word into syllables.

1. kindness

2. careful

3. helpful

4. seedless

5. clearly

6. healthful

Prepare for Suffixes

Here are nine common suffixes. How many words can you find that end with these suffixes? Write them in the columns. One word in each column has been done for you.

ful	less	ty
beautiful	worthless	royalty

ness	ly	ic
goodness	lonely	majestic

ist	er	ism
scientist	farmer	patriotism

A Bucketful of Suffixes

The suffix **ful** can be added to each word without changing the spelling of the root word. Write the correct word after each picture clue and add *ful* to the word. Use the words in the list to help you.

| harm | help | pain |
| spoon | bucket | hand |

1.

_____bucket_____+ ful

_____bucketful_____

2.

_____+ ful

_____

3.

_____+ ful

_____

4.

_____+ ful

_____

5.

_____+ ful

_____

6.

_____+ ful

_____

Sounds Greek to Me

The suffix **ic** is Greek and means *having to do with* or *containing.* Complete each sentence using a correct word from the list below.

antiseptic	scenic	terrific	scientific
angelic	majestic	volcanic	patriotic
	traffic	nomadic	

1. The travelers took the _____ route near the ocean.

2. My little baby brother looked _____ sleeping in his crib.

3. The circus was thrilling and _____ !

4. "America the Beautiful" is a _____ song.

5. The tall, _____ mountains were breathtaking.

6. The policeman directed the _____ at the sports stadium.

7. _____ people move frequently and do not have permanent homes.

8. The nurse put some _____ on my cut to prevent an infection.

9. Our class enjoyed working on a _____ problem.

10. The _____ gases escaped from Mt. St. Helens.

Double Anyone

Use the following clues to find words that contain consecutive double letters.

1. an animal _____

2. one of the four seasons _____

3. sport played in the fall _____

4. high level of understanding _____

5. to draw aimlessly _____

6. pirate _____

7. winged insect _____

8. animal with a long neck _____

9. person who asks for handouts _____

10. Earth's natural satellite _____

11. seasoning _____

12. flock of geese _____

13. move from side to side _____

14. to take for a period of time _____

15. grief, sadness _____

16. poem of fourteen lines _____

17. paper used in secret voting _____

18. great work of literature _____

Two of a Kind

Make a list of words that contain two of one letter of the alphabet. Examples include *aardvark*, *baby*, *cartoon*, and *dawdle*.

_____　　　_____

_____　　　_____

_____　　　_____

_____　　　_____

_____　　　_____

_____　　　_____

_____　　　_____

_____　　　_____

_____　　　_____

_____　　　_____

_____　　　_____

_____　　　_____

_____　　　_____

_____　　　_____

_____　　　_____

_____　　　_____

Begin and End

Each phrase below is a clue for an answer that begins and ends with the same letter.

1. antonym of low   h _ _ h

2. a type of boat   k _ _ _ k

3. the most abundant gas in

    the atmosphere   n _ _ _ _ _ _ n

4. children's sidewalk game   h _ _ _ _ _ _ _ h

5. the loss of memory   a _ _ _ _ _ a

6. opposite of minimum   m _ _ _ _ _ m

7. payment to stockholders   d _ _ _ _ _ _ d

8. a gas used in lighted signs   n _ _ n

9. one TV show in a series   e _ _ _ _ _ e

10. the fireplace floor   h _ _ _ _ h

11. blue-green   a _ _ a

12. a small infant   n _ _ _ _ _ n

13. a ray of moonlight   m _ _ _ _ _ _ m

14. a place for performances   a _ _ _ a

15. one who forms opinions and

    gives judgments   c _ _ _ _ c

16. a continent   A _ _ _ _ _ _ _ _ a

17. another continent   A _ _ _ _ _ _ _ a

18. another continent   A _ _ _ _ a

19. another continent   A _ _ a

20. another continent   E _ _ _ _ e

Anagrams

An **anagram** is a word formed by rearranging the letters of another word. Reorder the letters of each word below to make new words.

1. ocean _____

2. snap _____

3. Brian _____

4. owl _____

5. melon _____

6. pots _____

7. flea _____

8. ring _____

9. art _____

10. gum _____

11. heart _____

12. bat _____

13. paws _____

14. ape _____

15. tone _____

16. tap _____

17. stop _____

18. not _____

19. pore _____

20. wee _____

Four-Letter Words

Below are listed the middle letters of some four-letter words. Fill in the blanks to make four-letter words.

____ a n ____	____ i d ____
____ e a ____	____ o v ____
____ a r ____	____ a i ____
____ e l ____	____ a m ____
____ o a ____	____ f a ____
____ i k ____	____ a v ____
____ o l ____	____ o r ____
____ a r ____	____ v e ____
____ o u ____	____ y p ____
____ o o ____	____ a s ____

Here are the initial and final letters of some four-letter words. Fill in the blanks to make four-letter words.

c ____ ____ t	b ____ ____ d
s ____ ____ t	m ____ ____ t
d ____ ____ e	t ____ ____ e
r ____ ____ n	p ____ ____ t
l ____ ____ d	b ____ ____ t
f ____ ____ d	h ____ ____ e
s ____ ____ d	d ____ ____ r
s ____ ____ r	e ____ ____ n
a ____ ____ e	g ____ ____ e
h ____ ____ t	m ____ ____ t

Education

List all the words you can make from the letters in *education*. (**Note:** All of the words in your list must have at least 3 letters and each letter can be used only once in each word.)

_____	_____
_____	_____
_____	_____
_____	_____
_____	_____
_____	_____
_____	_____
_____	_____
_____	_____
_____	_____
_____	_____
_____	_____
_____	_____
_____	_____
_____	_____
_____	_____

Summertime

List words related to summertime that begin with each letter of the alphabet.

A _____

B _____

C _____

D _____

E _____

F _____

G _____

H _____

I _____

J _____

K _____

L _____

M _____

N _____

O _____

P _____

Q _____

R _____

S _____

T _____

U _____

V _____

W _____

X _____

Y _____

Z _____

Clipped Words

The following words are written in their shortened forms. Write the long forms of these words in the blanks to their right.

1. vet _____

2. tie _____

3. movie _____

4. champ _____

5. photo _____

6. copter _____

7. ref _____

8. mart _____

9. dorm _____

10. exam _____

11. ad _____

12. doc _____

13. lab _____

14. prom _____

15. flu _____

16. teen _____

17. gas _____

18. stat _____

19. lunch _____

20. mum _____

Shawn's Homework

Shawn wrote a report about a class trip to the zoo, but he had some trouble spelling. Help him to correct his paper before he gives it to his teacher. First, read his homework. Then circle the misspelled words and then write the correct spellings below each word on the lines provided.

> One day the forth-graid class went on a tripp
>
> too the zoo. They took a bus to get their. Then
>
> evryone joyned in groops to ture the zoo. The blew
>
> group went to sea the bares, the read group went to
>
> the seels, and the yelow grupe wawked to the monkie
>
> area. At nune, all the grupes meet for luncth. The
>
> children eight sandwitches and drank alot of watir.
>
> Aftar lunch, they saw a burd show in the zoo theeter.
>
> When the show wus ovur, it was thime to go home.
>
> The childern pilled into the buss and away thay went.
>
> They had a grate daye!

Abbreviations

An **abbreviation** is a shortened form of a word and is usually followed by a period. An abbreviation is never used by itself as a word. It is always used with other words or names.

- You **wouldn't** write . . .

  I live on the St. next to the park.

- You **would** write . . .

  I live at 4342 Pumpkin St. next to the park.

- And you **wouldn't** write . . .

  That's a Mt. I would like to climb.

- But you **would** write . . .

  Someday I want to climb Mt. Whitney.

List of some common abbreviations.

apt.	apartment	cont.	continued	Jr.	Junior
Aug.	August	Corp.	Corporation	kg	kilogram
Ave.	Avenue	Dec.	December	lb.	pound
Bldg.	Building	Dept.	Department	Oct.	October
Blvd.	Boulevard	ft.	feet	oz.	ounces
Capt.	Captain	in.	inches	Rd.	Road
cm	centimeters	Jan.	January	yr.	year

Match the abbreviations with the words they stand for. Then copy the abbreviation correctly. Don't forget periods!

Letter

_____ 1. Wed.

_____ 2. Mr.

_____ 3. St.

_____ 4. Dec.

_____ 5. U.S.

_____ 6. Capt.

_____ 7. tbs.

_____ 8. Blvd.

_____ 9. Aug.

_____ 10. Gov.

_____ 11. Jr.

_____ 12. gal.

_____ 13. Dr.

_____ 14. Tues.

_____ 15. yr.

Abbreviation

a. Boulevard _____

b. Mister _____

c. year_____

d. Governor_____

e. December _____

f. tablespoon _____

g. Tuesday_____

h. Street _____

i. gallon _____

j. Captain _____

k. Doctor _____

l. United States _____

m. Junior _____

n. Wednesday_____

o. August_____

More Abbreviations

Write the meaning of each abbreviation.

1. pres. _____

2. ASAP _____

3. adj. _____

4. lbs. _____

5. max. _____

6. etc. _____

7. Sept. _____

8. M.A. _____

9. I.O.U. _____

10. B.A. _____

11. c.o.d. _____

12. R.S.V.P. _____

13. S.A.S.E. _____

14. S.A. _____

15. bldg. _____

16. RR _____

17. prep. _____

18. hdqrs. _____

19. D.A. _____

20. D.S.T. _____

Alike Yet Different

Some words are spelled the same but are pronounced differently and have different meanings.

Examples

re′cord	record′	con′test	contest′
re′fuse	refuse′	close (clos)	close (cloz)
con′duct	conduct′	desert′	de′sert
con′tent	content′	read (rēd)	read (red)
sub′ject	subject′	ad′dress	address′

Choose the correct way of pronouncing the word in italics in each sentence below. Write the word at the end of the sentence and put the accent mark or vowel marks where they belong.

1. Our teacher will *record* us as we sing the national anthem. _____

2. We are studying about *desert* plants and animals. _____

3. Our little kitten was very *content* after we fed her. _____

4. Kim and I entered the art *contest*. _____

5. How can anyone *refuse* to do an act of kindness? _____

6. My mother *read* the directions for the recipe. _____

7. Please *close* the door gently. _____

8. Our *conduct* should be appropriate at all times. _____

9. What is your favorite *subject*? _____

10. My *address* is 221 Main Street. _____

Pronunciation Keys

When you use the dictionary, you will find guides to each word's pronunciation in parentheses. The dictionary will also give you a guide about how to read the pronunciations. However, if you know some basics, it will help. Use these tips.

A vowel written by itself makes the **short vowel** sound.

Examples: a, e, i, o, u

A vowel written with a straight line above it makes the **long vowel** sound.

Examples: ā, ē, ī, ō, ū

Read the pronunciation guides below. Using the two vowel tips above, write the words on the blanks.

1. mat _____

2. māt _____

3. tīn _____

4. tin _____

5. fed _____

6. fēd _____

7. us _____

8. ūs _____

9. mēt _____

10. met _____

Now it is your turn. Write two word pairs with pronunciation guides that change only by the long or short vowel sound.

_____   _____

_____   _____

What's the Word?

Read the pronunciation guides. Write the words.

1.	tāl	
2.	mōst	
3.	trās	
4.	hā´-zē	
5.	dō	
6.	dū´-əl	
7.	frā	
8.	trāl	
9.	re-plā´	
10.	whēl	
11.	mē´tər	
12.	mō´tər	
13.	gēs	
14.	chī´nə	
15.	luv	

Alphabetizing

Circle the words that are not in alphabetical order. Rewrite the words in their correct places.

ape	_____	put	_____
banana	_____	putt	_____
apple	_____	otter	_____
bear	_____	other	_____
cornhusk	_____	over	_____
carrot	_____	quitter	_____
cheese	_____	quit	_____
dandelion	_____	quilt	_____
dandy	_____	raise	_____
eggplant	_____	roast	_____
egg	_____	season	_____
grapes	_____	satisfy	_____
grass	_____	salt	_____
friend	_____	state	_____
frond	_____	town	_____
heaven	_____	tune	_____
hover	_____	tuna	_____
house	_____	umbrella	_____
ice	_____	under	_____
icicle	_____	underneath	_____
jump	_____	very	_____
juice	_____	voice	_____
kick	_____	violin	_____
kiss	_____	wisdom	_____
list	_____	wig	_____
laugh	_____	wonder	_____
limb	_____	xylophone	_____
mote	_____	yeast	_____
mother	_____	yesterday	_____
many	_____	yes	_____
neck	_____	zebra	_____
noise	_____	zoology	_____
pout	_____	zoo	_____

Alphabetical Order

Place these words in alphabetical order.

rover	jump	launch	scientist
river	light	cane	cell
moon	umbrella	candy	cello
cart	dog	same	dear
friend	sort	simple	deer
house	loop	grass	join
ghost	lope	grassy	tune
vest	game	lion	salt
silent	gamble	line	ghastly
tunnel	lunch	science	moan

_____ _____ _____ _____

_____ _____ _____ _____

_____ _____ _____ _____

_____ _____ _____ _____

_____ _____ _____ _____

_____ _____ _____ _____

_____ _____ _____ _____

_____ _____ _____ _____

_____ _____ _____ _____

_____ _____ _____ _____

What Does It Mean?

Many words have more than one meaning. When reading, you can use context clues to determine the meaning of a word in a sentence. Read the sentences below and then write the letter of the definition that shows how the underlined word is used in each sentence.

_____ 1. Tell me your <u>address</u> so I can find where you live.

      a. speak or write to

      b. manner of speech

      c. place where a person lives

_____ 2. Why do you <u>refuse</u> to come to the fair?

      a. decline to accept

      b. garbage

      c. decline to do

_____ 3. Lost in the <u>desert</u> for hours, the people were hot, hungry, and thirsty.

      a. dry, sandy wasteland

      b. abandon

      c. something deserved

_____ 4. The children at <u>play</u> were running and laughing with joy.

      a. put in motion

      b. taking part in a game or recreation

      c. a dramatic work

_____ 5. Are any cookies <u>left</u> for me?

      a. to the westward direction when one is facing north

      b. remaining

      c. departed

Define It

Each of these words has more than one meaning. Use a dictionary to write at least two meanings for each word.

1. **wind**

    a. _____

    b. _____

2. **close**

    a. _____

    b. _____

3. **record**

    a. _____

    b. _____

4. **part**

    a. _____

    b. _____

5. **conduct**

    a. _____

    b. _____

Choose one meaning for each word. Write the letter of the definition in the blank before each word. Then use the word in a sentence that shows the meaning.

_____ 1. **wind** _____

_____

_____ 2. **close** _____

_____

_____ 3. **record** _____

_____

_____ 4. **part** _____

_____

_____ 5. **conduct** _____

_____

Challenge: How many other words can you think of that have multiple meanings? Make a list and keep adding to it to see how many you can find.

Making Face Paint

Look at the directions for creating face paint found in the box below and then follow these directions:

A. Underline the important or key words in each sentence.

B. Number each step in the directions.

C. Draw a circle around each word that is a form of measurement.

D. Read the directions to a partner before you begin.

E. On another sheet of paper, make a list of the ingredients that you will need to do this project.

After creating a batch of face paint, work with a partner and paint your faces to look like zoo creatures.

In each container, mix 1 teaspoon of cold cream and 2 teaspoons of cornstarch.

Wash five small, empty food containers such as yogurt cartons or margarine tubs.

Add 1 teaspoon of water and a few drops of food coloring to each container. Blend carefully.

Be sure to use a different color for each container: blue, green, red, yellow, and brown.

Note: 1 teaspoon = 5 mL

Color This Design

Color this design so that no shapes of the same color touch one another. You may use only three colors. (*Hint:* Think out the design before you begin to color.)

Derek's Day

One type of graph that gives us information is called a circle graph. In a circle graph, you can show how things are divided into the parts of a whole.

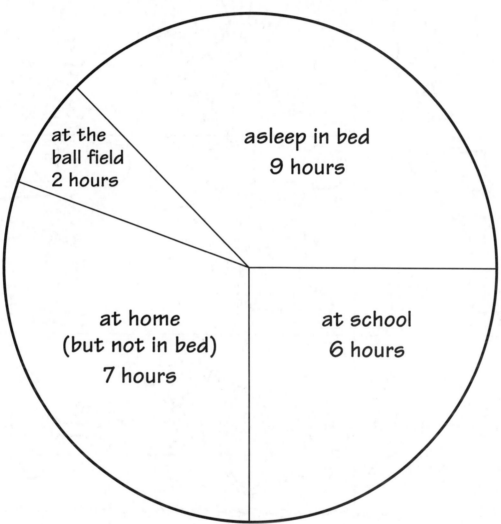

Derek's 24-Hour Day

- at the ball field 2 hours
- asleep in bed 9 hours
- at home (but not in bed) 7 hours
- at school 6 hours

- Color the place Derek spends 6 hours a day red.

- Color Derek's sleeping time blue.

- Color the time Derek spends on the ball field green.

- Color Derek's non-sleeping time at home yellow.

- On a separate paper, write some of the things you think Derek might do at home in seven hours.

Sequencing Pictures

Indicate the correct order of the pictures in each row by putting a 1, 2, or 3 in each box.

Reading Adventures

Read each story and then answer the questions.

Miles and Robin wanted to go to the
zoo. Their mother said they could go
after they finished their chores. First,
they cleaned their rooms. Next, they
mopped the kitchen floor. After that,
they washed the family's car. Finally,
they got ready to go to the zoo.

1. What did Miles and Robin do first? _____

   _____

2. What did the boys do after they mopped the floor?_____

   _____

3. What was the final thing the boys did? _____

   _____

Miles and Robin were on an
imaginary safari. First, their mother
gave them a map of the zoo. Then,
the boys went to the shark pool.
Next, they found their way to the tiger
cage. After that, they visited the wolf
den. Finally, they met their mother at
the alligator exhibit. Miles and Robin
had a busy afternoon!

4. What animal did the boys visit first? _____

   _____

5. Where did the boys go after they saw the tiger? _____

   _____

6. What did the boys do last? _____

   _____

Put Them in Order

Read the sentences. Rewrite them in a paragraph in the correct sequence.

I got out of bed and looked in the mirror.
I ran to my mother to show her what had happened.
She said, "Those seeds you swallowed yesterday have planted inside you."
I woke up one morning feeling strange.
Then she looked in the phone book for a good gardener to come over to trim me.
What a shock I got when I saw a plant growing out of my ears!
I am feeling better now, but I still have to water myself every day.

_____

_____

_____

_____

_____

_____

_____

_____

_____

Kelly's Week

Kelly was having a busy week. She wrote down a list of things to do each day, but her little brother accidentally ripped it up. Put the scraps back in order by writing Kelly's list below.

Write my book report on Thursday.

Call Janet on Saturday.

Bake cookies for school on Tuesday.

Practice the violin on Friday.

Go to baseball practice on Wednesday.

1. _____

_____

2. _____

_____

3. _____

_____

4. _____

_____

5. _____

_____

What Happened Next?

When you write about something that happened to you or something that you do, it must be in the right time order. Another name for this is **chronology**. The things you write about in a paragraph should usually be in *chronological* (time) *order* to make sense.

Here are some lists of events that are out of order. Put them into time (chronological) order by marking them from first (1) to last (5). The first one has been done for you.

A.

2	eat breakfast
1	get up
5	go to school
4	go out the door
3	brush teeth

E.

_____ slap your arm

_____ see a mosquito

_____ feel a bite

_____ hear a buzz

_____ scratch a bump

B.

_____ bait a hook

_____ clean a fish

_____ eat a fish

_____ catch a fish

_____ cook a fish

F.

_____ buy popcorn

_____ leave the theater

_____ stand in line

_____ buy a ticket

_____ watch a movie

C.

_____ mail the letter

_____ put the letter in envelope

_____ write the letter

_____ wait for an answer

_____ seal the letter

G.

_____ find an old Halloween mask

_____ clean up your room

_____ sneak up on your brother

_____ put it on

_____ jump out at him

D.

_____ write a book report

_____ click on word processing

_____ turn on printer

_____ turn on computer

_____ print book report

H.

_____ snap on the leash

_____ pull your dog back home

_____ get the leash

_____ whistle for your dog

_____ walk your dog

What's the Point?

Each paragraph has a series of sentences in a special order. The sentences work together to develop a single idea. Each of the sentences in a paragraph must relate to the main idea.

Cross out the idea in each list that does not relate to the main idea. The main idea is in boldface type.

1.   **inside my house**

   kitchen   football field
   bedroom   bathroom
   living room   attic

2.   **colors**

   red   yellow
   blue   bird
   green   purple

3.   **countries**

   Canada   Mexico
   United States   Beverly Hills
   France   Australia

4.   **homework**

   erasers   paper
   fortune cookies   pencils
   books   crayons

5.   **tools**

   screwdriver   diving board
   hammer   saw
   wrench   pliers

6.   **food**

   beans   spinach
   towels   tomatoes
   corn   bread

7.   **sports**

   soccer   tennis
   baseball   basketball
   scissors   golf

8.   **animals**

   dogs   cats
   flowers   horses
   cows   mice

9.   **musical instruments**

   piano   harmonica
   tomato soup   guitar
   drums   trumpet

10.   **clothes**

   jackets   spaghetti
   pants   socks
   sweaters   shirts

Extension: Choose one of the topics above and write an outline for a paragraph using four subtopics. For example . . .

Clothes

A. jackets
   1. sports jackets
   2. dressy jackets
B. pants
   1. leggings
   2. jeans
   3. dress pants

C. socks
   1. sweatsocks
   2. wool socks
D. sweaters
   1. _____
   2. _____

Writing Text for Pictures

Write a sentence under each picture that gives the main idea of the picture.

What's It About?

Draw a picture that shows the main idea of each paragraph.

The baby chicks began to hatch very slowly. We could see their tiny beaks poking through the cracked shells, and we could hear their tiny peeping. We held our breaths and watched with excitement with every crack they made. It would be so wonderful to see the chicks when they are fully hatched!

The three friends went camping and had a great time. Danny pitched the tent, and Carl hunted for firewood. Larry laid out all the supplies and made sure they were not disturbing any animal's home. Everyone helped, and that made the trip even better.

Practice on Main Idea

Read the paragraph below. Circle the details that help you find the main idea. Then color the magnifying glass that has the main idea that makes sense.

Clues At the Zoo

Juan and Julie want to work at the city zoo when they grow up. They read books about animals from all around the world so that they can learn about animals. Every Saturday, Julie and Juan visit the zoo around feeding time. It is interesting to see what the animals eat and how they feed their young. Many of the animals eat vegetables and fruits. Julie and Juan know that they must be good at science if they want to work at the zoo. Zoology is the science that deals with animals and animal life. A person who studies zoology is called a zoologist. A zoologist must be smart and hardworking.

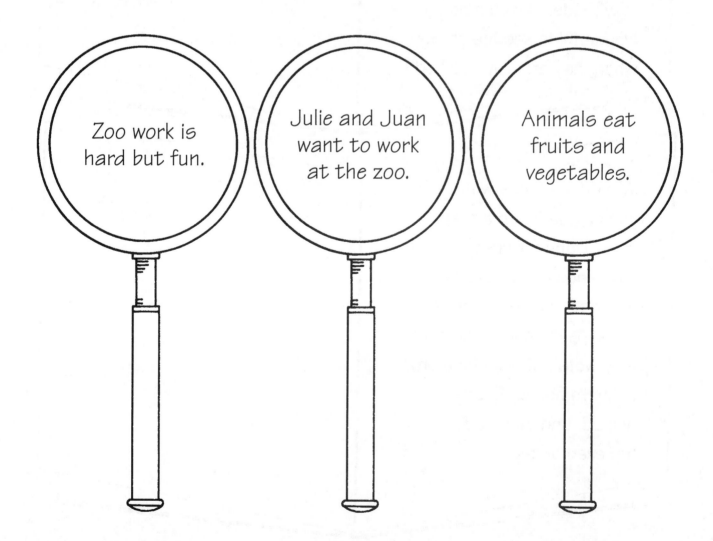

Zoo work is hard but fun.

Julie and Juan want to work at the zoo.

Animals eat fruits and vegetables.

Main Idea of a Paragraph

It is easy to write the main idea of a paragraph. Read the paragraph carefully and answer the three Ws. You do not need to use complete sentences here. Then make a good sentence out of your answers. Read your new sentence carefully to make sure it makes sense. Practice with the paragraph found below.

> Lola loved to watch the big, beautiful birds from South America. She stared at the parrots' bright green wings as the birds flew gracefully in their giant bird cage. Lola laughed when they called to each other with loud, squeaky voices. The parrots were Lola's favorite animals at the zoo.

1. Who? _____

2. What? _____

3 Why? _____

4. Write a sentence using your answers.

_____

_____

Check to make sure your sentence is complete.

1. Does your sentence make sense? ☐

2. Does it start with a capital letter? ☐

3. Does it end with a period? ☐

Main Idea Story Parts

Read each story and then write a sentence that best tells the main idea.

The students in Mrs. Lee's class were having a great time at the Riverside Zoo. As they were walking to visit the chimpanzees again, Mrs. Lee suddenly stopped. "Is anyone wearing a watch?" she asked. "I'm afraid that mine has stopped."

Amanda looked at her watch. "It's 1:40," she said.

Mrs. Lee's eyes opened wide. "Oh, no! We were supposed to meet Mrs. Miles' class at 1:30. We're late!"

Mrs. Lee and her students began running for the bus.

Main idea: _____

One of the penguins was ready to play. He waddled up the icy hill as fast as he could. Then he flopped onto his stomach and slid down. Some of the penguins were eating lunch. They swallowed the fish as quickly as the zookeeper could empty the big buckets of food. A few of the penguins were sleeping quietly.

The children watched the penguins for a long time. When it was time to leave the exhibit, all of the children were sad to go. Many of the children liked the penguins exhibit best.

Main idea: _____

Max

Read the story and then answer the questions.

A very young boy named Max visited the nature center last Monday. While he was there, several penguin eggs hatched. Max was one of the first people to see the baby penguins because he happened to be nearby when the babies were born. Max was very happy to be a part of this exciting event.

1. Who is the story about?

   _____

2. What does he do?

   _____

   _____

3. Why does he do this?

   _____

   _____

4. Use your answers to write a main idea sentence.

   _____

   _____

5. Draw a picture of the main idea.

George Washington

Read the story and then answer the questions.

One of the greatest leaders in American history is George Washington. He was a general in the Revolutionary War against the British. The people of the new nation were proud of the work he did during the war, and many people thought he would be the best person to lead the country as its first president. General Washington became president for eight years in all, and he is still remembered as an excellent leader.

1. Who is the paragraph about?

   _____

2. What is this person known as?

   _____

   _____

3. Why is this person known in this way?

   _____

   _____

4. Use your answers to write a main idea sentence.

   _____

   _____

5. Write a short paragraph with additional information that you have discovered about George Washington.

   _____

   _____

   _____

   _____

   _____

   _____

My Dream

Read the story and then answer the questions.

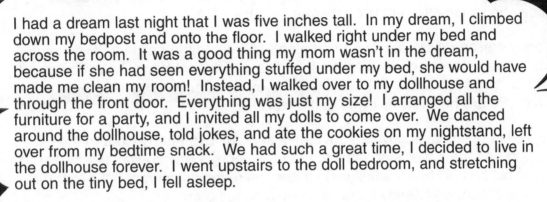

I had a dream last night that I was five inches tall. In my dream, I climbed down my bedpost and onto the floor. I walked right under my bed and across the room. It was a good thing my mom wasn't in the dream, because if she had seen everything stuffed under my bed, she would have made me clean my room! Instead, I walked over to my dollhouse and through the front door. Everything was just my size! I arranged all the furniture for a party, and I invited all my dolls to come over. We danced around the dollhouse, told jokes, and ate the cookies on my nightstand, left over from my bedtime snack. We had such a great time, I decided to live in the dollhouse forever. I went upstairs to the doll bedroom, and stretching out on the tiny bed, I fell asleep.

When I woke up from my dream, I smiled as I remembered it. Then I looked inside my dollhouse and wondered. How did those cookie crumbs get in there?

1. How does the girl get down from her bed? _____

_____

2. What is the girl glad her mother does not see? _____

_____

3. What does the girl do to get ready for the party? _____

_____

4. What do the partygoers eat? _____

_____

5. What surprises the girl when she wakes from her dream? _____

_____

The Big Game

Read the story and then answer the questions.

Kenny couldn't wait. Today was the day, his big chance. For weeks he had been practicing every day, throwing to anyone who was willing. Now he would get to do what he had been preparing for since the season began. Today he would pitch in the big game!

Kenny dressed excitedly and raced on his bicycle to the ballpark. His coach was already there, ready for warmups. The coach sent Kenny to the bullpen, and he began to throw. He could feel the excitement building with every pitch. Before he knew it, it was game time!

While his teammates covered the bases and outfield, Kenny went to the mound. As the batter stepped into the box, Kenny knew he was ready. He threw his first pitch, a fastball that hit just inside the strike zone. "Strike!" the umpire called, and Kenny knew this would be his game.

Nine innings later, Kenny found he was right! His team won, 12 to 8, and Kenny was named Most Valuable Player. It was a game to remember!

1. Why couldn't Kenny wait? _____

_____

2. What had Kenny been practicing? _____

_____

3. How did Kenny get to the ballpark? _____

_____

4. What did Kenny do first thing at the ballpark? _____

_____

5. What was Kenny named? _____

_____

Inferences

When you use clues to draw conclusions about things, you are making inferences. Read the short paragraph below and make an inference.

> "What a mess! It's raining cats and dogs out there! I could barely get through the flood in front of the walkway," Karly complained as she walked into the classroom, soaking wet.

Is Karly (1) happy about the rain, (2) annoyed about the rain, or (3) worried about the rain?

If you said annoyed, you are right. List three clues in the paragraph that tell you that Karly is annoyed.

1. _____

2. _____

3. _____

Now it is your turn. Write a short paragraph that shows Karly is either happy or worried about the rain.

_____

_____

_____

_____

_____

_____

_____

_____

_____

_____

_____

_____

Making Inferences

Read the examples and answer the questions that follow each example. (Remember, when you use clues to draw conclusions about things, you are inferring.)

"It sure is dark in here. Could we turn on some lights?" asked Wendy and Jack.

"The Fun House is too spooky!" said Jack as he walked through it.

"I'm ready to go on the Ferris wheel," said Wendy.

1. What can you infer? _____

   _____

2. What clues did you find to prove you inferred correctly?

   _____

   _____

"I am not jealous of your new dress," said Mary. "I don't like that color on me anyway. My mother buys me more expensive things than that. I think the material looks like it would rip easily and not wash well. Where did you buy it? Was that the only one they had left?" asked Mary.

1. What can you infer? _____

   _____

2. What clues did you find to prove you inferred correctly?

   _____

   _____

Marta and Janis

Read the story. Then use the lines under the story to write how the two friends are the same and how they are different from each other.

Marta and Janis are both eight years old. They have been best friends for two years, even though Marta does not speak much English. Marta is from Mexico. She speaks Spanish very well, a language that Janis does not understand. Marta is teaching Janis to speak Spanish, and Janis is helping Marta to speak better English.

Every afternoon, the girls do their homework together. They munch on their favorite snack, popcorn. Sometimes Janis has to bring her little brother along. He colors in his coloring book while the girls study. Marta loves little Pete, and she wishes she had a baby brother or sister.

After they finish their homework, Marta and Janis go to the city park. Marta takes her skates. She is a wonderful skater. Janis brings her scooter. She loves to ride. When Pete comes along, all the children swing and slide. They all enjoy that! It is good to have a best friend!

1. How are Marta and Janis alike?

_____

_____

_____

_____

_____

2. How are Marta and Janis different?

_____

_____

_____

_____

_____

Drawing Conclusions

Read the sentences below and then answer the questions.

Answer

1. I live on a farm. I have feathers and wings. I wake up the farm in the morning. What am I?	
2. You watch me in a large building. There are a screen and a projector. People eat popcorn and drink soda while I am playing. What am I?	
3. Some people use me to write, other people use me to play games, and many people use me to find information and to send messages to each other. I can be found in many homes and most businesses. What am I?	
4. I grow from the ground. I smell sweet. My stem has thorns, but I am beautiful. What am I?	
5. I make beautiful sounds. I have a long neck and strings. Some people use a pick to play me. They strum my strings, and the sound vibrates. What am I?	

What Next?

Finish the story below by drawing a cartoon and writing a conclusion.

"What's that?" Cindy asked as a bright light shone overhead.

"I don't know for sure, but I know it's not a helicopter or an airplane," Liz answered.

"Do you think it's dangerous?" Cindy wondered out loud.

"I don't want to stay around to find out!" Liz yelled as the bright light began to land.

Conclusion

_____

_____

_____

_____

_____

Cause and Effect

Everything that happens (**effect**) is caused by something else (**cause**). Read the effects in the first column. Write a cause in the second column.

Effect	Cause
1. spilled milk	
2. torn jeans	
3. trampled flowers	
4. flat tire	
7. happy children	
8. frustration	
9. coldness	
10. tiredness	
11. wealth	
12. peace	
13. tears	
14. illness	
15. friendship	

What's the Effect?

Whatever makes something happen is called the **cause**. Read the causes in the first column. Write a reasonable effect of each in the second column.

Cause	Effect
1. dog running through house	
2. children playing	
3. woman pruning flowers	
4. driving fast	
5. forgetting an appointment	
6. eating poorly	
7. watching eight hours of television	
8. wearing sandals and shorts on a cold day	
9. spending too much money	
10. oversleeping	
11. forgetting to return a book to the library	
12. losing your wallet	

Facts and Opinions

When you write a research paper, you must be very careful to stick to the facts. A research paper is written to give people information that is true or that can be proven true.
Is this a fact? **"France is the best place in the world to live."** Whether you agree or not, it is just someone's opinion. It is not a fact.

In the blanks before each sentence below, write **F** for fact or **O** for opinion.

> **Fact**
> Many plants have thorns.

> **Opinion**
> Thorny plants are not good in gardens.

_____ 1. The moon orbits the earth.

_____ 2. The moon is inspirational to all who see it.

_____ 3. A banana tastes disgusting.

_____ 4. A banana is a fruit.

_____ 5. Abraham Lincoln was killed.

_____ 6. Abraham Lincoln was the best president.

_____ 7. Canada has the most beautiful lakes in the world.

_____ 8. Canada has many lakes.

_____ 9. Red and yellow mixed together make orange.

_____ 10. Orange is the prettiest color.

Now write one fact and one opinion about your school.

1. Fact: _____

2. Opinion: _____

Evaluating Bias

Facts tell only what can be proven. Biased statements tell a person's **opinion**. Underline the biased statements below.

1. Lions roar loudly.

2. Pigs are the laziest of all animals.

3. Horses must be brushed often to keep them clean.

4. Dogs are better pets than cats.

5. The Riverside Zoo was built three years ago.

6. More than 400 animals live in the Riverside Zoo.

7. The Riverside Zoo is the best zoo in the world.

8. The emperor penguin is the most interesting animal to watch.

9. Snakes should not be allowed at the zoo because they frighten visitors.

10. Polar bears are large, white animals.

Tone

The **tone** of a story is the feeling it has and the feeling it makes the reader have. A tone can be happy, sad, excited, fearful, or many others.

Word Bank

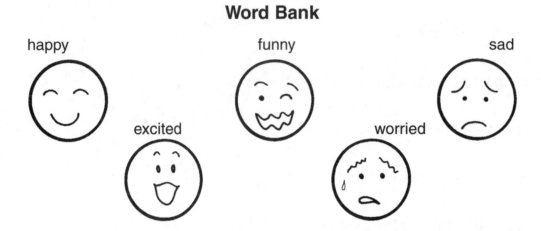

Read each group of sentences below. Then write the tone each group of sentences sets. Choose from the words in the word bank.

1. Wow! Today is my birthday. I know it will be a great day. We are having a chocolate cake and are playing lots of games. I can hardly wait until my friends arrive.

   Tone: _____

2. I can't believe my best friend is moving away. I want to cry. Even the sky looks gray and rainy today. Nothing will ever be the same without my friend.

   Tone: _____

3. Can a pig learn tricks? My pet pig, Sally, can roll over and shake hands. Or should I say shake snouts? She is a funny pig who really likes to "hog the show."

   Tone: _____

4. I can't believe our arithmetic test is today. I forgot to study, and I don't understand multiplication. I just know I will fail this test. This could ruin my math grade. Oh, why didn't I study last night?

   Tone: _____

5. It is a beautiful day today! The sun is shining, the birds are singing, and the air smells sweet and fresh. It feels good to be alive!

   Tone: _____

Identifying Tone

Read the sentences. Each one suggests a mood or feeling. This is called the **tone**. On the blanks, write the tone of each.

1. The sunset fell in beautiful shades of orange, pink, and yellow.

   _____

2. The children ran through the yard like puppies at play.

   _____

3. Rain ran down the windowsill while the twins watched, sighing and cupping their chins in their hands.

   _____

4. The fans went wild, shouting and stomping their feet while he rounded the bases for another home run.

   _____

5. The two bighorn sheep clashed their horns together angrily.

   _____

6. The tiny baby screamed and cried until she fell asleep.

   _____

7. The fingernails screeched loudly across the chalkboard.

   _____

8. Slam! The basketball swished through the hoop to make the winning point!

   _____

9. The roar of the engines drowned their voices as they tried to shout to each other at the racetrack.

   _____

10. Oh, I wish I had a million dollars!

    _____

Identifying the Speaker

Read the story and answer the questions below.

Tracy had a big surprise when he took the trash out one night. He saw a small, furry animal hanging upside down in the trash can. "Get out of there!" yelled Tracy.

"What is going on?" called his father.

"Raccoons are hunting in our garbage," said the boy. He went back into the house and got a broom to chase the raccoons away. But when he came back, the furry raccoons were already gone. "I guess I'd better make sure that the lid is on tightly," he said.

1. How many speakers are in the story? _____

2. Who are the speakers? _____

3. Who said that he should make sure that the lid was on tightly?

   _____

4. How do you know Tracy is a boy? _____

   _____

First-Person Voice

Read the entry in the diary below. The author, Ashley, recorded her thoughts and feelings. She used the words *I* and *me* often. When she reads her diary again, she will know that she means herself when she reads those pronouns. When you read something with the words *I* or *me*, meaning the author, that is written in what is called the **voice of the first person**. The diary entry below is written in the voice of the first person.

Dear Diary,

I wonder how the animals in the zoo feel when the weather is this cold? I worry that their fur and feathers will not keep them warm enough. It bothers me to think that the animals may be cold. Tomorrow I will ask my teacher about how animals keep warm.

Ashley

Put a check after the sentences below that are written in the first person.

1. I am happy about our trip to the zoo. _____

2. The three girls watched the polar bear dance. _____

3. The zookeeper let me hold the owl. _____

4. I could feel the smooth skin of the snake. _____

5. The old monkey fussed at the younger ones. _____

Third-Person Voice

Read the story below.

> Two kangaroos shared a cage at the zoo. Matilda kept her side of the cage as neat a pin. Elsie never picked up her belongings. Matilda often thought that Elsie was lazy about housekeeping, but she never fussed at Elsie about it. The two kangaroos lived peacefully together.

The author wrote about the kangaroos as if she were an invisible person in their cage. They did not know she was there, but she pretended to see and hear them all of the time. She could even pretend to know what they were thinking. When an author writes about someone else and pretends to know what he says, does, and thinks, the author is writing in the **voice of the third person**. Remember, when the author is the person speaking in the story, that is the **voice of the first person**. Write a **1** by the sentences written in the first person. Write a **3** by the sentences written in the third in person.

1. _____ The boys were excited about the new movie.

2. _____ I am anxious to go to the zoo.

3. _____ Please walk with me to the hippopotamus exhibit.

4. _____ Seven seals swam happily back and forth in the pool.

Pronoun Referents

Read each set of sentences. Notice the words in bold. They are pronouns. Then answer the questions.

1. Alicia would like a new doll. **She** hopes to get one for her birthday. Who is she?

   _____

2. Luke and Chris are playing baseball. **They** want to become professional ball players one day. Who are they?

   _____

3. The movers came to take our furniture away. **They** will deliver it to our new house. Who are they?

   _____

4. I played with my dog, Sam, yesterday. **He** loves to play catch. Who is he?

   _____

5. **You and I** should go to the movies. There is a new movie we would really like to see. Who are we?

   _____

6. My computer is broken. **It** will not turn on when I push the power button. What is it?

   _____

7. Tom and his sisters went next door to play. **He** was told to keep an eye on **them**. Who is he? Who does them refer to?

   _____

   _____

Idioms

Idioms are expressions whose meanings are different from the literal ones. Explain what the idioms below actually mean.

1. When Angelica said, "That movie **took my breath away**," she meant _____

   _____

2. "When Dad finally **put his foot down**, my brother started to do better in school," said

   Boris. What Boris meant was _____

   _____

3. Dana stood and said, "I guess I'll **hit the road** now." What Dana meant was

   _____

4. When Mario said that he was a bit **under the weather** last weekend, he meant that

   _____

5. When Nicholas said that he **slept like a log** last night, he meant _____

   _____

6. "I'll be **in the doghouse** for sure," exclaimed Roberto. What Roberto really meant was

   _____

7. "**Hold your horses**," remarked the police officer. The police officer meant _____

   _____

8. When Ryan asked Patricia, "Are you **getting cold feet**?" he was actually asking

   _____

9. If Grandpa loves **to spin a yarn**, he _____

   _____

10. When Leslie says that she is **in the dark** about what's going on, she means

    _____

More Idioms

Idioms are expressions with meanings which are different from the literal ones. Explain what the idioms below actually mean.

1. Dinner's on the house. _____

    _____

2. John got up on the wrong side of the bed. _____

    _____

3. My cousin has a green thumb. _____

    _____

4. Money burns a hole in my pocket. _____

    _____

5. He should mend fences before leaving. _____

    _____

6. Cathy didn't have the hang of it yet. _____

    _____

7. Mother told us to straighten up the house. _____

    _____

8. Dad always gets up with the chickens. _____

    _____

9. The sick child wasn't out of the woods yet. _____

    _____

10. Crystal was down in the dumps all day. _____

    _____

Analogies

Analogies are comparisons. Complete each analogy below.

Example: <u>Ear</u> is to <u>hearing</u> as <u>eye</u> is to <u>seeing</u>.

1. Cardinals is to St. Louis as Dodgers is to _____

2. A.M. is to before noon as P.M. is to _____

3. Three is to triangle as eight is to _____

4. Tear is to tore as see is to _____

5. Springfield is to Illinois as Austin is to _____

6. Carpet is to floor as bedspread is to _____

7. Go is to green as stop is to _____

8. Purple is to grapes as red is to _____

9. Ghost is to Halloween as bunny is to_____

10. Son is to dad as daughter is to _____

11. Jelly is to toast as syrup is to_____

12. Ear is to hear as eye is to _____

13. Oink is to pig as cluck is to_____

14. Mississippi River is to U.S. as Nile River is to _____

15. Clock is to time as thermometer is to_____

16. V is to 5 as C is to _____

17. Up is to down as ceiling is to _____

18. Car is to driver as plane is to _____

19. Sleep is to tired as eat is to _____

20. Bird is to nest as bee is to _____

More Analogies

Analogies are comparisons. Complete each analogy below. An example has been done for you.

Example: <u>Kangaroo</u> is to <u>joey</u> as <u>bear</u> is to <u>cub</u>.

1. See is to eye as _____ is to nose.

2. Ping-Pong® is to paddle as _____ is to racquet.

3. Bob is to Robert as Liz is to _____.

4. Writer is to story as poet is to _____ .

5. Car is to _____ as plane is to pilot.

6. Kennedy is to John as _____ is to Theodore.

7. Glove is to hand as boot is to _____ .

8. Hammer is to _____ as pen is to writer.

9. Bear is to _____ as bee is to hive.

10. _____ is to picture as curtain is to window.

11. Sing is to song as _____ is to book.

12. _____ are to teeth as contact lenses are to eyes.

13. Left is to _____ as top is to bottom.

14. _____ is to pool as jog is to road.

15. Wrist is to hand as _____ is to foot.

16. Hammer is to nail as _____ is to screw.

17. Paw is to dog as _____ is to fish.

18. Meat is to beef as _____ is to apple.

19. _____ is to pig as neigh is to horse.

20. Princess is to _____ as prince is to king.

Still More Analogies

Analogies are comparisons. Complete each analogy below. An example has been done for you.

Example: <u>Wide</u> is to <u>narrow</u> as <u>tall</u> is to <u>short</u>.

1. Big is to _____ as large is to small.

2. Hat is to head as shoe is to _____ .

3. Bird is to nest as _____ is to hive.

4. Rug is to _____ as curtain is to window.

5. _____ is to road as boat is to lake.

6. Boy is to man as _____ is to woman.

7. _____ is to room as gate is to yard.

8. Sleep is to tired as _____ is to hungry.

9. Zoo is to animals as library is to _____ .

10. Floor is to _____ as ceiling is to top.

11. _____ is to grass as blue is to sky.

12. Belt is to _____ as bracelet is to wrist.

13. Car is to driver as airplane is to _____ .

14. Book is to _____ as television is to watch.

15. Grape is to vine as peach is to _____ .

16. Ear is to hearing as _____ is to seeing.

17. _____ is to day as dusk is to dawn.

18. Thanksgiving is to November as Christmas is to _____ .

19. Calf is to cow as _____ is to lion.

20. _____ is to uncle as niece is to aunt.

All Together Now

Each set of words belongs to a different group. Classify the group by writing its name on the blank.

1. Easter, Yom Kippur, and Thankgiving are _____.

2. Shawna, Kate, and Mariella are _____.

3. Denmark, Greece, and Cuba are _____.

4. Bananas, apples, and strawberries are _____.

5. Cows, chickens, and sheep are _____.

6. Violet, plum, and lavender are _____.

7. Pencils, pens, and markers are _____.

8. Goofy, Mickey, and Donald are _____.

9. Clowns, trapeze artists, and the ringmaster are _____.

10. Stanford, Princeton, and Yale are _____.

11. Nile, Colorado, and Thames are _____.

12. East, south, and northwest are _____.

13. "Little Boy Blue," "Mary Had a Little Lamb," and "Little Miss Muffet" are _____.

14. Van Gogh, Michaelangelo, and Da Vinci are _____.

15. Lincoln, Kennedy, and Reagan are _____.

16. Three, fourteen, and twenty-nine _____.

17. A, Q, and Z are _____.

18 Donut, cookie, and pie are _____.

19. Jones, Lopez, and Chang are _____.

20. Hammer, saw, and wrench are _____.

Categories

Place the following words in each of the categories below. There are seven for each.

bassoon	harp	peccary	sloth
carnation	impatiens	meerkat	snipe
strawberry	iris	phoebe	sweet William
cello	kayaking	pineapple	triathlon
crocus	lacrosse	Ping-Pong	toucan
cummerbund	loganberry	poncho	trousers
flute	mandolin	primrose	trumpet
football	mango	quetzal	tux
gardenia	moccasin	quince	violin
gown	papaya	rugby	
guava	parka	soccer	

Animals

_____
_____
_____
_____
_____
_____
_____

Fruits

_____
_____
_____
_____
_____
_____
_____

Flowers

_____
_____
_____
_____
_____
_____
_____

Sports

_____
_____
_____
_____
_____
_____
_____

Instruments

_____
_____
_____
_____
_____
_____
_____

Clothing

_____
_____
_____
_____
_____
_____
_____

Get Rid of the Details

Read the paragraph below. It has too many details to be a summary. You must decide which words or phrases are not important enough to be in a short summary. Cross out the words or phrases that are not important details. To create a summarizing paragraph, copy the sentences and words you did not cross out.

Every animal has babies. Sometimes the mother takes care of the baby until it can take care of itself. Baby animals are cute. Sometimes the whole group of animals care for the babies. Baby bears are called cubs. The cubs like to eat honey. Baby animals must eat. Mothers and fathers protect their babies. Some baby animals, like kangaroos, live in pouches. Other baby animals travel on their mothers' backs. Possums and monkeys carry babies on their backs. Baby animals are fun to watch.

Summary

_____

_____

_____

_____

_____

_____

  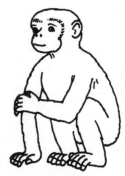

Summarize

Read the paragraph and then follow the directions below.

Butterflies are beautiful insects. They flutter around in the spring air. They rest upon the tulips and daisies. Butterflies can be dark brown, bright yellow, orange, blue, or any number of colors. They begin life as caterpillars. Then, they spin silky covers called cocoons. Inside the cocoon, the caterpillar turns into a butterfly. Butterflies help to spread pollen from one flower to another, so butterflies are helpful as well as beautiful.

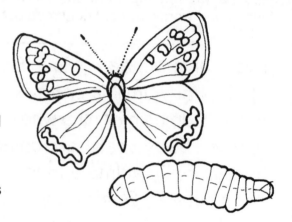

You can shorten a paragraph through summarizing. When you summarize, you include the main idea and the most important details, leaving out everything else. Summarize the paragraph above.

_____

_____

_____

_____

_____

_____

_____

_____

_____

Practice Summarizing

Write a paragraph about your favorite animal. You can use the facts from your science book or an encyclopedia. Be sure to begin each sentence with a capital letter and end each sentence with a period.

_____

_____

_____

_____

_____

_____

Write two sentences that summarize your paragraph. Give the main idea and the most important details.

_____

_____

_____

Your Day

On the blanks, write everything you can remember doing today in chronological order (beginning with waking up).

_____   _____

_____   _____

_____   _____

_____   _____

_____   _____

_____   _____

Now, take what you wrote above, and group the ideas together under three or four headings (such as "getting ready" or "being at school"). Write your group headings here.

_____   _____

_____   _____

_____   _____

Finally, write a summary of your day, using your group names. Write the summary in no more than three sentences.

_____

_____

_____

_____

_____

Pick a Part

Read a book and describe your favorite parts.

The part that was the funniest was _____

_____

_____

_____

The part that was the saddest was _____

_____

_____

_____

The part that was the most unbelievable was _____

_____

_____

_____

The part I liked best was _____

_____

because _____

_____

_____

Read All About It

Find an article that you think is interesting in a newspaper or magazine. Read the article and then answer these questions.

What is the topic of the article?

_____

_____

_____

_____

_____

What new things did you learn about the topic?

_____

_____

_____

_____

What else would you like to learn about the topic?

_____

_____

_____

_____

Why is this article interesting?

_____

_____

_____

_____

Character Web

You can see this is a special kind of web. It is a **character web.**

Read a book. Draw a picture of the main character in the center circle. In each of the spaces, answer the question about the character.

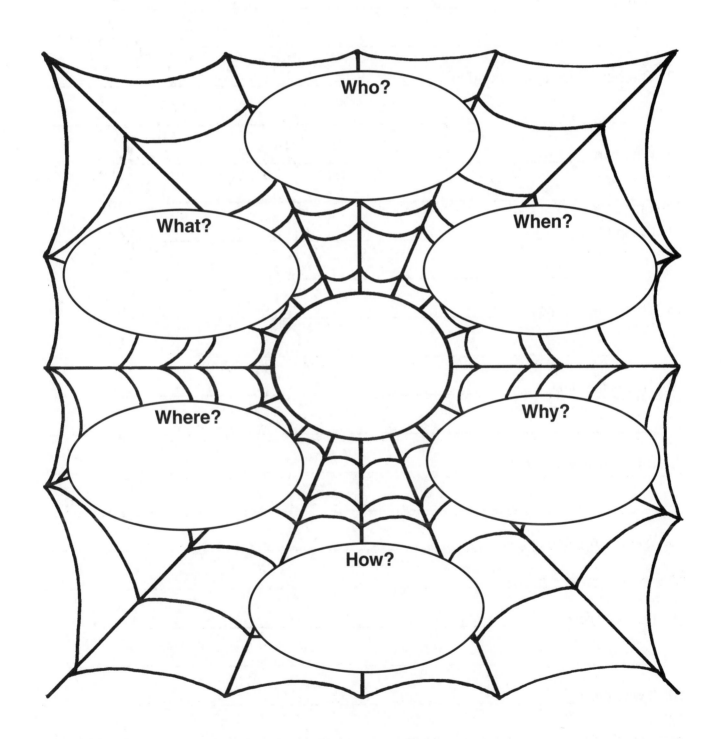

Complete the Sentences

Sentences begin with capital letters and end with a period, exclamation point, or question mark. Every sentence must also have a subject and a predicate. Here are some incomplete sentences. Complete them, being sure to add punctuation at the end.

1. Sandy cried when she _____

   _____

2. The best place in the world to _____

   _____

3. Who can _____

   _____

4. I wish I had _____

   _____

5. There aren't many _____

   _____

6. This is the best _____

   _____

7. It's times like this that _____

   _____

8. When are you going to _____

   _____

9. I can't believe _____

   _____

10. It was the _____

    _____

Write a Sentence

Write a sentence for each picture.

1. _____
_____

2. _____
_____

3. _____
_____

4. _____
_____

5. _____
_____

6. _____
_____

7. _____
_____

8. _____
_____

Start with a Noun and a Verb

Draw a line to match each noun to a verb. (**Note:** Change the tense of each verb to best fit each sentence.)

Nouns	Verbs
children	climb
squirrel	sleep
sun	blare
orchestra	run
wind	crumble
television	shout
father	shine
teenager	color
horse	play
paint	blow

Write a sentence for each noun-verb pair.

1. _____

2. _____

3. _____

4. _____

5. _____

6. _____

7. _____

8. _____

9. _____

10. _____

Sentence Expansions

The sentences below are complete because they each have a subject and a predicate. However, they are the simplest sentences possible. Add words to each sentence to make it more interesting.

1. Vine climbed. _____

   _____

2. Cat leapt. _____

   _____

3. Cake burned. _____

   _____

4. Donkey brayed._____

   _____

5. Toddler fell. _____

   _____

6. Lightning struck. _____

   _____

7. Mother called._____

   _____

8. Truck stopped. _____

   _____

What Do You Think?

You have learned that every sentence must begin with a capital letter and end with a period, question mark, or exclamation point. You have also learned that a sentence must be a complete thought. A sentence needs to have enough information to make sense. It needs to ask you a complete question or tell you a complete idea. There are 10 incomplete sentences on this page. Rewrite the sentences to make them complete.

1. Jennifer wants to

   _____

2. Yesterday, while it was raining, I

   _____

3. Do you

   _____

4. all the way down the hill

   _____

5. is very annoying

   _____

6. I wish I had

   _____

7. Did they try

   _____

8. Watch out for the

   _____

9. is a big, scary monster

   _____

10. jumped into the spaghetti

   _____

Word Muncher

Here are some sentences that are missing subjects or predicates. Choose a subject or predicate from the box to complete each sentence. Then, on the line before each number, write a **P** if you added a predicate or an **S** if you added a subject to the sentence. The first one is done for you.

The following subjects and predicates may be used more than once.

My teacher	An ugly grasshopper	fell on my toe.
The mail carrier	The tree	is growling.
My kitten	has an attitude.	is singing in an opera.
has a cute little hat.	is crying.	is really an alien.
A ladybug	climbs on the furniture.	is covered in stripes.
Uncle Gerald	is lost in space.	was under the house.
My sister	Dinner	is as big as Australia.
A cute little baby	My bed	is a spy.
A suitcase	drove over the hills	The doctor
is very gross.	ran on the playground.	floats away.
is drooling.	snores.	is purple with polka dots.

___S___ 1. _____ My Kitten _____ sat on the birthday cake.

_____ 2. _____ ate worms for breakfast.

_____ 3. Laurie _____ .

_____ 4. _____ slipped on a banana peel.

_____ 5. Mrs. Crabapple _____ .

_____ 6. _____ is a big, hairy beast.

_____ 7. A giant elephant _____ .

_____ 8. My little brother _____ .

_____ 9. The grizzly bear _____ .

_____ 10. _____ is very heavy.

_____ 11. _____ has the measles.

_____ 12. A jet plane _____ .

_____ 13. _____ is green.

_____ 14. My science book _____ .

_____ 15. _____ is growing blue fur.

Combining Sentences

Combine these simple sentences into compound sentences. **Compound sentences** will combine two or more complete sentences by using commas and conjunctions.

1. Liz and Tanya are best friends. They do everything together. They want to be sisters.

   _____

   _____

2. Michael has three favorite sports. He likes to play baseball. He likes to play basketball.
   He likes to bowl.

   _____

   _____

   _____

3. You can do many things with a computer. You can use it to write. You can use a
   computer to play games. You can use a computer to create art.

   _____

   _____

   _____

4. The tiger walked through the savanna. She was looking for food. She wanted to feed
   her young.

   _____

   _____

5. The children were out of school for the day. They played a game together. They had fun.

   _____

   _____

6. Two fish live in the fishbowl. There are colorful rocks and a small castle in the fishbowl.
   The fish swim through the castle.

   _____

   _____

Get to the Point

In the paragraph below, cross out the sentences that are not related to the main idea.

I love food, but I do not like to cook. First of all, I am not very good at cooking. I cut myself, I burn food, and I spill things that stain all my clothes. My clothes are nice things that cost most of my money, even though I usually get them on sale. The other day I stained a nice, corduroy shirt which made me really mad. It was robin's egg blue. Then there is something about the ingredients that is a great mystery to me. I usually like mysteries—in fact, I check out mysteries each week at the library. I can follow a recipe very closely, but it never comes out right. The food might be too salty, too sweet, or just too weird. And then there's the mess. I need to clean up my room, too. It is such a big mess right now. The food sticks to pots and pans and stains the sink. There is a really strange stain on the ceiling in the hallway; it looks like an octopus. The floor, the dog, and I get covered in flour or onion juice. When I get finished with all that labor, I'm anxious to taste my masterpiece, but it is always a disappointment, and there are so many dishes that I don't have time to go out and get something really good to eat! I should just give up cooking altogether!

Rewrite the corrected paragraph on the lines below.

_____

_____

_____

_____

_____

_____

_____

_____

_____

_____

How About a Little Help?

A topic sentence does not work alone to explain the main idea of a paragraph. **Helping sentences**, also known as **body sentences** or **supporting sentences**, work to help the topic sentence. They help make the main idea clear.

There are four main ideas listed on this page. In the word bank below, find the helping or supporting ideas for each main idea. The main idea would be included in your topic sentence. The helping ideas would be included in your body sentences.

Word Bank

lemons	ovens	frying pans
tires	dandelions	bumpers
ears	knees	thumbs
refrigerators	steering wheels	bananas

---

1. Main Idea: **car parts**

   Supporting Ideas: _____

   _____

   _____

2. Main Idea: **kitchen things**

   Supporting Ideas: _____

   _____

   _____

3. Main Idea: **body parts**

   Supporting Ideas: _____

   _____

   _____

4. Main Idea: **yellow things**

   Supporting Ideas: _____

   _____

   _____

Extension: Take the four categories above and write four paragraphs, each with a topic sentence and three supporting sentences.

Missing Parts

Here is a paragraph that is missing some parts. The three reasons that support the topic sentence are missing. Can you fill them in? Be sure to use complete sentences.

I would not like to lose my favorite toy for three reasons. The first reason is _____

_____

_____

Another reason is _____

_____

_____

Finally, if I lost my favorite toy, _____

_____

I want to keep my favorite toy!

◆   ◆   ◆   ◆   ◆   ◆   ◆

Try writing another paragraph.

I should receive an "A" on this assignment for three reasons. _____

_____

_____

_____

_____

_____

_____

Extension: Try some more on a separate piece of paper:

- I would like to build a fort in my backyard for three reasons.
- My (sister/brother/cousin/friend) is from another planet, and there are four items of evidence to prove this.
- I (do, do not) like cats for four reasons.
- There are three reasons I (would, would not) eat a snail—even for one hundred dollars.

And Then . . .

Sentences in paragraphs need to make sense with each other. They need to be connected. The words that help connect ideas between sentences are called **transitions**. These transitions help make your writing easier to understand.

Using the transitions in the parentheses, connect the sentences below. Write the new sentences in paragraph form. Be sure to indent and make sense.

1. I'll eat a salad.

   I feel like eating a hot, cheesy pizza.

   I've been eating too many pizzas lately.

   (**however**, **so**, **today**)

   Today, I feel like eating a hot, cheesy pizza.

   However, _____

   so _____

   _____

2. She made me do my homework.

   My mother rushed in and unplugged my stereo.

   I was enjoying music in my room.

   (**suddenly**, **after that**)

   _____

   _____

   _____

   _____

3. I sprinkle everything with nuts.

   I pour fudge or strawberry sauce over the scoops.

   I love to make ice-cream sundaes.

   I scoop ice cream into bowls.

   (**first**, **then**, **finally**)

   _____

   _____

   _____

   _____

Extension: Using old newspapers or magazines, look at paragraphs and see what kinds of transitions are used to make the writing smoother. Use a highlighter to mark the transitions. Listen to the radio or television news. In these programs they call transitions segues ("segways"). Listen for segues and write down your favorites.

This Is the Story

One kind of paragraph is called *narrative*. A **narrative paragraph** gives the details of an experience or event in story form. It explains what happens in a natural time order. You have probably written a narrative paragraph before, but you just didn't know what to call it. You have definitely spoken a narrative paragraph. On the first day of school, you probably went home and told someone all about it in chronological order. In each of the paragraphs below, choose one of the main ideas in parentheses or use one of your own. Use another piece of paper if you need more room.

The first time I ever (*rode a bike, cooked, babysat*) was a total disaster.

First, _____

_____

Next, _____

_____

Then, _____

_____

Finally,_____

_____

✦   ✦   ✦   ✦   ✦   ✦   ✦

I had never been (*more embarrassed, more angry, more excited*) in my life!

_____

_____

_____

_____

_____

✦   ✦   ✦   ✦   ✦   ✦   ✦

On (*my first day at school, my last birthday, my last vacation*), I_____

_____

_____

_____

_____

_____

_____

Start Explaining

One type of paragraph is the *expository paragraph*. **Expository writing** gives facts, explains ideas, or gives directions. Below are some expository paragraph topics. Choose one and on the lines below, write one paragraph for the topic that you choose.

❑ Explain how you wash your hair.

❑ Give the facts about your favorite baseball team.

❑ Explain how you make a peanut butter sandwich.

❑ Explain how to ride a bike.

❑ Tell what abilities are needed to participate in your favorite sport.

❑ Explain how to write a poem.

❑ Tell why you like hamburgers.

_____

_____

_____

_____

_____

_____

_____

_____

_____

_____

Give Us a Description

Another kind of paragraph is the *descriptive paragraph*. A **descriptive paragraph** gives a clear picture of a person, place, idea, or thing. Think of the word picture whenever you are writing a descriptive paragraph. Your writing needs to make a word picture. A good way to make a word picture is to use as many of the five senses as you can in your description.

Imagine that you have gone to a strange new mall with your family. You turn to look at something, and when you look back your family is no longer in view. Everywhere you look there are strangers in an unfamiliar mall. You feel anxious and a little bit afraid. Fill in the lines below with descriptions.

❑ What do you see?

_____

_____

❑ What do you hear?

_____

_____

❑ What do you smell?

_____

_____

❑ What do you touch?

_____

_____

❑ What do you taste?

_____

_____

❑ How do you feel?

_____

_____

On another piece of paper, write a descriptive paragraph about what you are experiencing and how you are feeling. Use details to describe your main idea. Be sure to use the things you described above to write your paragraph.

I Will Convince You

A **persuasive paragraph** is what you write when you express an opinion and try to convince the reader that your opinion is correct. Think of how you try to persuade a parent to buy your favorite cereal or a new pair of shoes that you are convinced you must have. You may be convinced, but you will need to work hard to persuade others. To persuade, you will need lots of *examples, details*, and *evidence to prove your point*.

Here is an example of a persuasive paragraph.

> Everybody needs to have a pet. Have you ever noticed that people who do not have pets are grouchier than those who do? If they were greeted whenever they came home by a furry creature thrilled to see them, they would be a lot less grouchy. A pet is affectionate and a good companion. Pets like to snuggle and be with people. Also, pets are always positive. If you give them a special treat, they act as if you've given them the world's largest diamond or the fastest car. They shudder with joy, leap, and prance. If you've had a hard day, they still greet you with enthusiasm. They don't care what you do. You can be a complete failure, and they still treat you as if you are a king or queen. Pets love you unconditionally. If you forget to feed them, they forgive you the moment you remember. Pets are also good safety devices. They can scare away strangers. They can warn you if there is a fire or something wrong inside or outside the house. All they ask in return is a bag of food, some water, and some TLC (tender, loving care). If everybody had a pet, everybody would go around smiling.

Choose a topic below or create your own topic and, on a separate piece of paper, write a persuasive paragraph. Remember to be as convincing as you can.

- ❏ Pets are a waste of time and money.
- ❏ We should continue to explore space.
- ❏ Space exploration is not a good use of our money.
- ❏ Libraries are invaluable.
- ❏ Bookstores are better than libraries.
- ❏ People should always have dessert.
- ❏ Desserts should be banned.
- ❏ Everybody should play a sport.
- ❏ Sports are overrated.
- ❏ Jewelry is fun.
- ❏ Jewelry is expensive.

- ❏ Students should wear uniforms to school.
- ❏ Students should be allowed to dress the way they want.
- ❏ We should have more zoos.
- ❏ We should do away with zoos.
- ❏ More people should be eating vegetables.
- ❏ Vegetables should be banned from the earth.
- ❏ Amusement parks should be free.
- ❏ People need to pay to get into amusement parks.

In My Opinion . . .

An **opinion paragraph** is similar to a persuasive paragraph. In each, you have a point to make. With an opinion paragraph, you need to focus on your opinion, state what you think about something, and support your point with your reasons for having such an opinion. You don't need to convince the reader that you are right. You do need to be clear enough that the reader understands why you have the opinion. For practice, fill in the blanks below to complete this opinion paragraph.

There are several reasons why I (like, dislike) spiders. First, _____

_____

_____

Second, _____

_____

_____.

The most important reason why I _____ spiders is

_____

_____.

Therefore, _____

_____

_____.

Write an opinion paragraph below about an important belief or opinion you have. Your opinion will be your topic sentence. Then support your belief with strong reasons, saving the most important reason for last. Finally, sum up your opinion in the last sentence. (Some ideas for your opinion paragraph are *war, allowance, homework, religion, birthdays, equal rights, families, violence,* and *television*.)

_____

_____

_____

_____

_____

_____

_____

_____

Define This!

A **definitive paragraph** is a very important piece of writing because when we define things, we help others to understand our writing, our viewpoint, our opinion, and the point we wish to make. Usually when people think of a definition, they think of the dictionary. That's fine. Dictionaries are important and necessary, but do not use one for this activity. Instead, look inside your imagination and see if you can create a personal definition for each word below. Keep these questions in mind to help you write your definitions.

1. **What is it?**

2. **What does it look like?**

3. **How does it feel?**

4. **What does it smell like?**

5. **Does it have a sound?**

6. **What does it do?**

7. **How is it used?**

8. **How does it make me feel?**

9. **Does it have a purpose?**

10. **What thing or things is it completely different from or similar to?**

Now, do your best to complete the following beginning definitions. Each one will take several sentences to do a good job.

A shoe is_____

_____

_____

_____

A watermelon is _____

_____

_____

_____

Happiness is_____

_____

_____

_____

_____

_____

When I Grow Up

What kind of a career do you want to have when you grow up? There are many career ideas on this page. Choose one of these ideas or one of your own that you would like for a career. Write a paragraph about your choice.

❏ farmer	❏ forest ranger
❏ architect	❏ doctor
❏ teacher	❏ engineer
❏ juggler	❏ astronaut
❏ nurse	❏ animal trainer
❏ musician	❏ builder
❏ police officer	❏ writer
❏ baseball player	❏ lawyer
❏ clown	❏ manager
❏ artist	❏ designer
❏ actor	❏ photographer
❏ pilot	❏ firefighter
❏ computer scientist	❏ filmmaker
❏ veterinarian	❏ chef

My Career

I would like to be _____

for three reasons. The first reason is_____

_____

Another reason is _____

_____.

Finally, I would like to be _____

_____

because _____

_____

_____

_____

Sticky Glue

You placed your assignment on the table. You did not know that the table had sticky-icky glue on it. When you picked up your paragraph, ugh! Now you will need to rewrite it. First, choose your topic.

> I learned how to . . .(*rollerskate, rollerblade, bicycle, sew, surf, ski, eat an artichoke, skateboard, paint, ride a horse, plant a garden, snowboard, bake cookies, etc.*).

Now rewrite your sticky assignment by completing the following parts that are still "readable."

I just learned how to _____

_____!

The first thing I did was _____

_____.

Next, I _____

_____.

After that, I _____

_____.

Finally, I _____

_____.

_____ is easy now!

Paragraph Starters

Use these paragraph starters when you need inspiration while practicing paragraph writing. You might want to use some of these ideas for writing an essay, a report, or a story.

Gorillas make good pets.	If I were my teacher, here are three things I would do.
There are many uses for popcorn.	It's a good idea for all students to invite the principal to dinner.
Collecting bugs is an interesting hobby.	Kids should be allowed to drive when they are 10 years old.
There are many things shaped like a circle.	There are lots of reasons why I am glad to be a member of my family.
I would like to be invisible.	I really like math (science, English, social studies, etc.).
I have three favorite foods.	I should have my own room.
I know my brother (sister) is an alien.	I deserve a raise in my allowance.
I would like to join the circus.	Eating is one of my favorite activities.
If I could stop time, there are three things I would do.	We should remember to wash our hands.
I would make a great president.	I would like to visit Mars.
I would like a giraffe for a pet.	It's a good idea to learn a foreign language.
It would be a good idea to build a roller-coaster in my backyard.	I love music.
Airplanes are not a good idea.	I would like to remodel my house.

Getting Your Paragraph Organized

Use this form to help you organize your paragraphs. Write a topic sentence in the circle at the top. Write three supporting ideas in the rectangles. Write your conclusion sentence in the triangle. Use these sentences to build your paragraph, adding any other words and details that you need to make it complete.

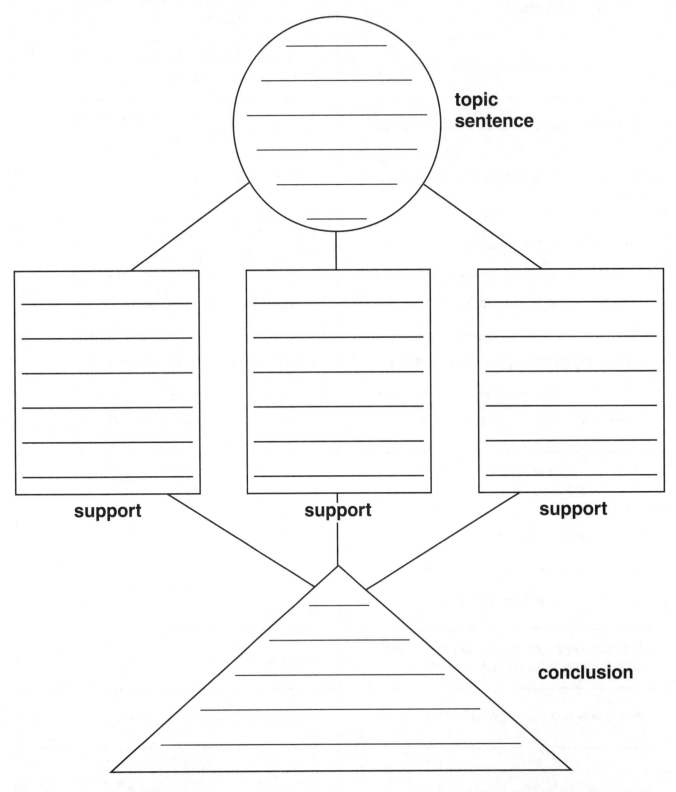

topic sentence

support   **support**   **support**

conclusion

Writing by Sense

One of the best ways to write descriptively is to use your senses. Think about how something looks, smells, sounds, tastes, and feels, and then write about it, keeping those senses in mind. For example, instead of writing, "The flower smells nice," you can write, "The sweet nectar of the flowers tickles my nose." This gives an idea of exactly how the flower smells. For another example, instead of writing, "The puppies are cute," write, "The playful puppies roll over each other and tumble into a ball of fur and pink noses." This gives an idea of exactly how the puppies look. Sentences that use the senses to describe are much more interesting to read, and they make the images seem real for the reader.

Follow each direction below to write a sentence using sense writing.

1. Describe how a skyscraper **looks**._____

   _____

   _____

2. Describe how a freshly mowed lawn **smells**._____

   _____

   _____

3. Describe how a yipping dog **sounds**. _____

   _____

   _____

4. Describe how a lemon **tastes**. _____

   _____

   _____

5. Describe how a kitten **feels**._____

   _____

   _____

Similes

A **simile** is a figure of speech in which two things are compared by using the words *like* or *as*, such as in "The ice was as smooth as glass." Complete the following similes.

1. As deep as _____

2. As dark as _____

3. As hard as _____

4. As quiet as _____

5. As flat as _____

6. As sweet as _____

7. As silly as _____

8. As hot as _____

9. As soft as _____

10. As slow as _____

11. As strong as _____

12. As cold as _____

13. As loud as _____

14. As clear as _____

15. As bright as _____

More Similes

A **simile** is a figure of speech in which two unlike things are compared using the words *like* or *as*. (**Example:** He moved as quick as a wink.) Complete the following common similes.

1. As fresh as _____

2. As white as _____

3. As wise as _____

4. As fit as _____

5. As tall as _____

6. As lazy as _____

7. As hard as _____

8. As stubborn as _____

9. As cute as _____

10. As black as _____

11. As blind as _____

12. As happy as _____

13. As cool as _____

14. As stiff as _____

15. As clean as _____

16. As limp as _____

17. As busy as _____

18. As light as _____

19. As good as _____

20. As pretty as _____

Metaphors

Metaphors compare two different things without using *like* or *as*. (**Example:** His feet are giant boulders.) Use comparison words to complete the metaphors.

1. The clown is a _____

2. The bird is a _____

3. The elephant is a _____

4. The falcon is a _____

5. The moon was _____

6. The snow was _____

7. The baby was _____

8. The game was _____

9. The thunder and lightning were _____

10. The field was _____

11. The sand is _____

12. The river is _____

13. The grandparents were _____

14. The dress is _____

15. That hat is _____

Writing Stories in Parts

Use the next two pages to create a story about one of the following topics. Write the story in three parts: introduction, body, and conclusion.

- The Day That I Got Lost
- My Pet Saved the Day
- When I Grow Up

- Best Friends Have an Adventure
- My Adventures in Space
- The Most Unforgettable Day of My Life

Part One: introduction or beginning

_____

_____

_____

_____

_____

_____

_____

Part Two: body or middle of the story

_____

_____

_____

_____

_____

_____

_____

Writing Stories in Parts (cont.)

Part Two (*cont.*):

_____

_____

_____

_____

Part Three: conclusion or ending of story

_____

_____

_____

_____

_____

_____

Check yourself.

1. Did you begin the story with an attention-getter? ☐

2. In the beginning did you tell who was in the story? ☐

3. Did you give lots of details in the middle? ☐

4. Did you bring the story to a close in the ending? ☐

5. Did you check your spelling? ☐

6. Did you write neatly? ☐

Story Time!

Can you use your imagination to make a flow chart for a story? A story about a fierce dragon is started for you. Make up the rest of the story about this dragon. The last box is your ending. Write your words in the boxes on the left and draw some pictures in the boxes on the right that will go with your words.

Once upon a time, there was a very fierce dragon.	
The End	

Circus Balloon

Finish the story below. Use good descriptive words in your story.

A man from the circus filled the boy's large, red balloon with helium and tied it to a long, white string. The boy held the string tight in his hand and walked over to see the enormous, gray elephant. All of a sudden, a brisk wind . . .

_____

_____

_____

_____

_____

_____

_____

_____

_____

_____

_____

_____

Dreams

Describe a dream that you once had and draw a picture to go with it. Be sure to write complete sentences with subjects and predicates.

_____

_____

_____

_____

_____

_____

_____

_____

What a Success!

Imagine that one day you become very famous. Write a story about the success that brings you fame. Give your story a title. In the story, explain how and why you became famous. Also tell about what other important things you might do in the future.

_____

_____

_____

_____

_____

_____

_____

_____

_____

_____

_____

_____

_____

_____

_____

_____

_____

_____

_____

_____

Letter Review

Trace the letters and then practice them on your own.

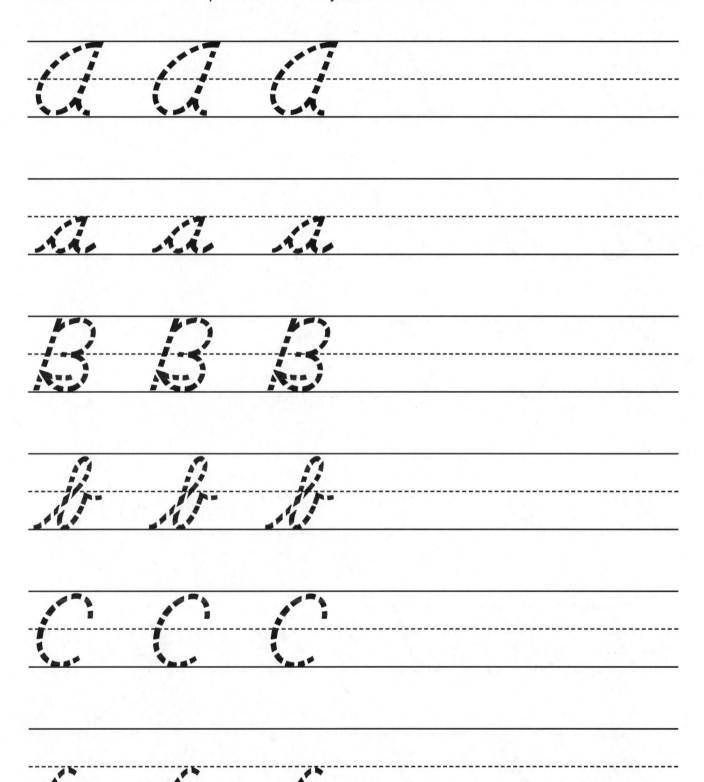

Letter Review (cont.)

Trace the letters and then practice them on your own.

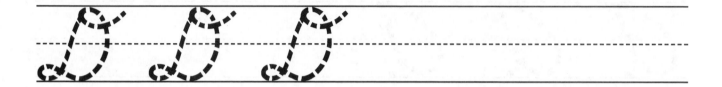

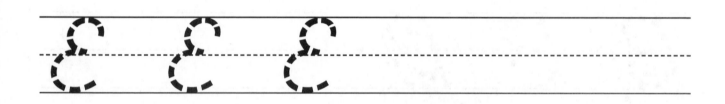

Letter Review (cont.)

Trace the letters and then practice them on your own.

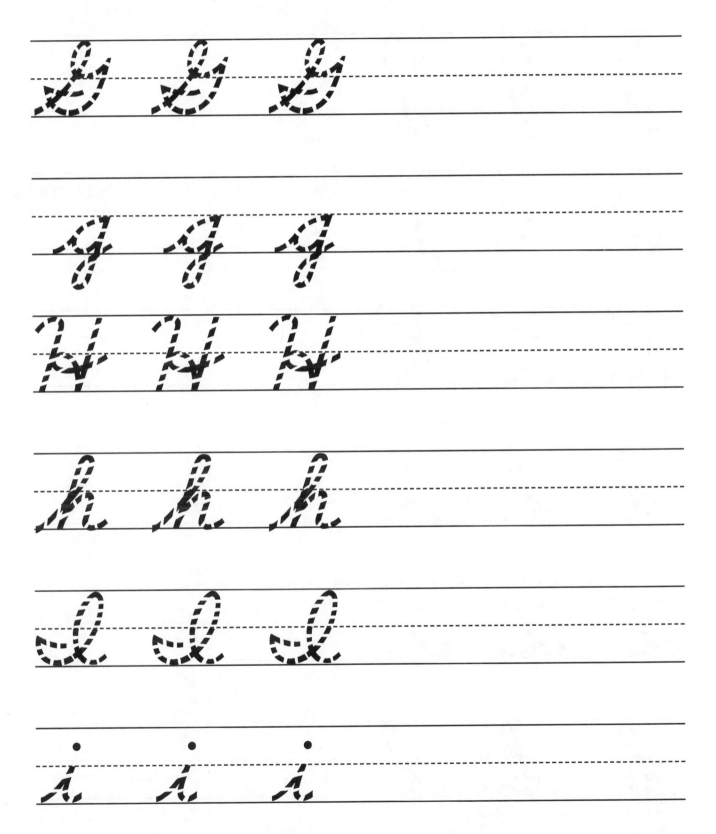

Letter Review (cont.)

Trace the letters and then practice them on your own.

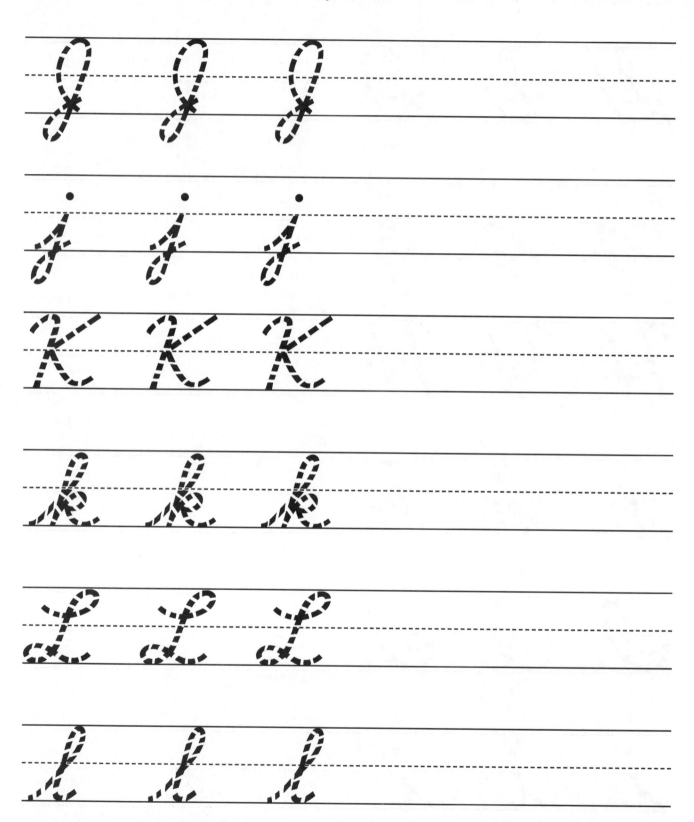

Letter Review (cont.)

Trace the letters and then practice them on your own.

Letter Review (cont.)

Trace the letters and then practice them on your own.

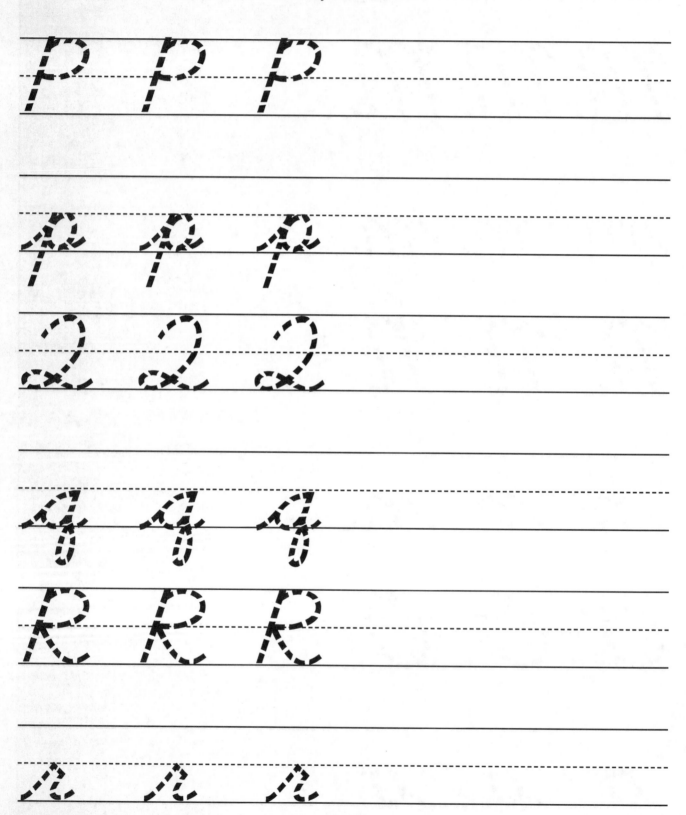

Letter Review (cont.)

Trace the letters and then practice them on your own.

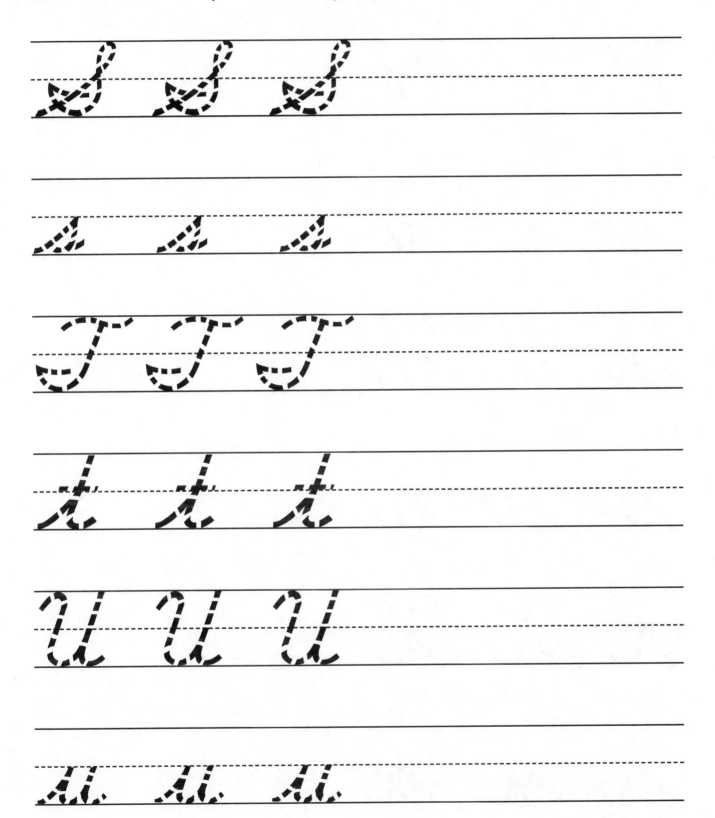

Letter Review (cont.)

Trace the letters and then practice them on your own.

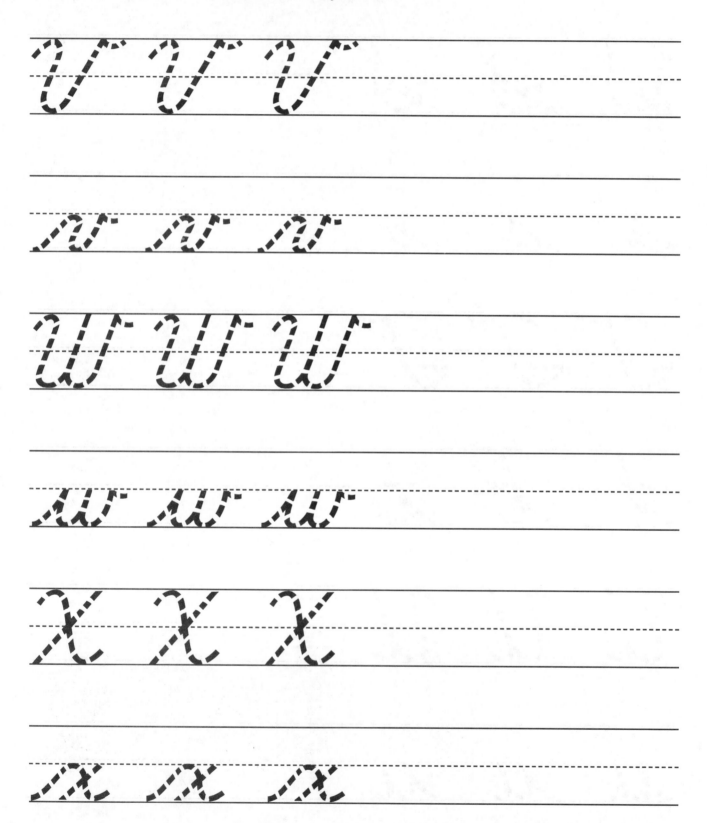

Letter Review (cont.)

Trace the letters and then practice them on your own.

Add It Up

Find the sums for the addition problems below.

1.	$1 + 3 =$ _____	16.	$3 + 2 =$ _____
2.	$5 + 8 =$ _____	17.	$2 + 0 =$ _____
3.	$3 + 7 =$ _____	18.	$6 + 2 =$ _____
4.	$9 + 3 =$ _____	19.	$9 + 5 =$ _____
5.	$6 + 1 =$ _____	20.	$1 + 6 =$ _____
6.	$2 + 4 =$ _____	21.	$8 + 9 =$ _____
7.	$1 + 2 =$ _____	22.	$7 + 6 =$ _____
8.	$8 + 0 =$ _____	23.	$9 + 4 =$ _____
9.	$0 + 3 =$ _____	24.	$6 + 8 =$ _____
10.	$4 + 6 =$ _____	25.	$5 + 5 =$ _____
11.	$7 + 7 =$ _____	26.	$5 + 4 =$ _____
12.	$3 + 5 =$ _____	27.	$4 + 8 =$ _____
13.	$4 + 2 =$ _____	28.	$2 + 8 =$ _____
14.	$9 + 2 =$ _____	29.	$3 + 6 =$ _____
15.	$6 + 9 =$ _____	30.	$0 + 9 =$ _____

Mouse in the House

Cross out each answer in the computer as you solve the problems.

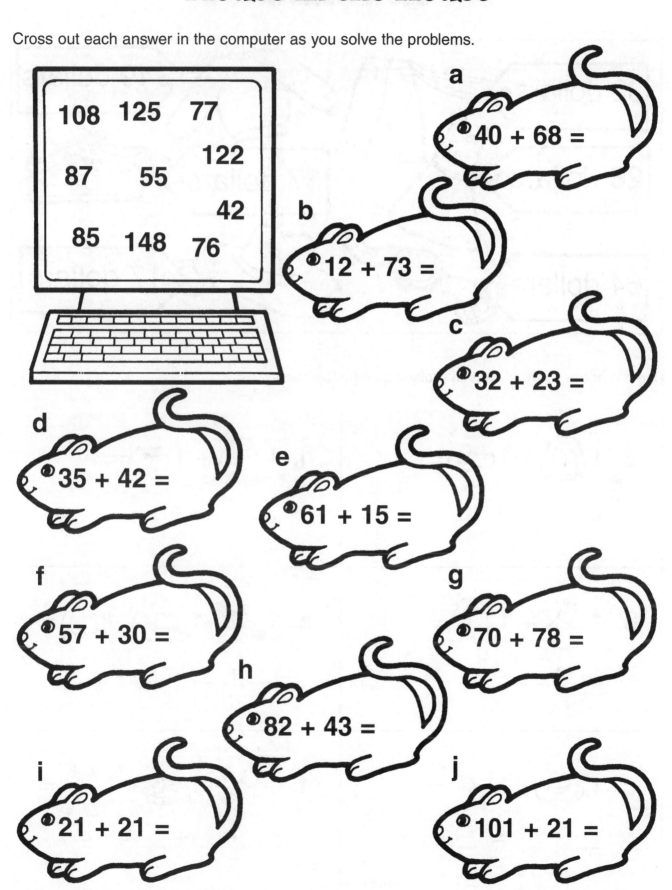

108   125   77

122

87   55

42

85   148   76

a 40 + 68 =

b 12 + 73 =

c 32 + 23 =

d 35 + 42 =

e 61 + 15 =

f 57 + 30 =

g 70 + 78 =

h 82 + 43 =

i 21 + 21 =

j 101 + 21 =

How Much?

Use the prices to write addition problems. Find the sums.

a. 1 ⟨sweater⟩ + 1 ⟨shoes⟩ =

___ + ___ = ___

d. 1 ⟨jeans⟩ + 1 ⟨shoes⟩ =

___ + ___ = ___

b. 1 ⟨dress⟩ + 1 ⟨jeans⟩ =

___ + ___ = ___

e. 1 ⟨watch⟩ +1 ⟨hat⟩ + 1 ⟨sweater⟩ =

___ + ___ + ___ = ___

c. 1 ⟨hat⟩ + 1 ⟨watch⟩ =

___ + ___ = ___

f. 1 ⟨dress⟩ +1 ⟨shoes⟩ + 1 ⟨jeans⟩ =

___ + ___ + ___ = ___

Word Problems

Read each word problem. Write the number sentence it shows. Find the sum.

a

In the forest, Lisa counted 83 pine trees, 24 spider webs, and 16 chipmunks. How many things did she count in all?

b

In Bill's classroom there are 47 pencils, 21 pieces of chalk, and 33 bottles of glue. How many supplies are there in all?

c

At the park, Carla counted 14 ducks, 32 children, and 24 roller skates. How many things did she count in all?

d

James counted 36 stars one night, 42 stars the next, and 87 on the third night. How many stars did he count in all?

Sum It Up

Find the sums.

a. 11 + 50	**g.** 69 + 12	**m.** 69 + 16	**s.** 36 + 13
b. 64 + 42	**h.** 72 + 38	**n.** 71 + 59	**t.** 29 + 80
c. 24 + 93	**i.** 48 + 18	**o.** 13 + 68	**u.** 51 + 17
d. 17 + 20	**j.** 52 + 11	**p.** 41 + 96	**v.** 19 + 91
e. 58 + 72	**k.** 15 + 19	**q.** 82 + 30	**w.** 31 + 46
f. 67 + 14	**l.** 31 + 62	**r.** 93 + 90	**x.** 87 + 43

Add Three

Find the sums.

a. 39 57 + 47	**g.** 39 12 + 72	**m.** 26 71 + 59	**s.** 17 79 + 54
b. 33 75 + 23	**h.** 51 24 + 88	**n.** 52 30 + 18	**t.** 39 95 + 48
c. 21 53 + 17	**i.** 42 84 + 19	**o.** 13 38 + 42	**u.** 27 77 + 70
d. 42 26 + 49	**j.** 23 14 + 92	**p.** 52 38 + 42	**v.** 59 44 + 16
e. 68 62 + 56	**k.** 84 36 + 65	**q.** 52 66 + 83	**w.** 51 36 + 24
f. 61 33 + 63	**l.** 34 42 + 30	**r.** 98 61 + 15	**x.** 67 73 + 30

Addition Challenge

Find the sums for the problems below.

1.	684	2.	485	3.	321
	792		379		831
	+ 123		+ 369		+ 700

4.	680	5.	304	6.	421
	303		262		489
	+ 425		+ 750		+ 492

7.	278	8.	409	9.	557
	915		501		627
	+ 964		+ 961		+ 990

10.	863	11.	645	12.	789
	777		129		528
	+ 421		+ 300		+ 450

Cup o' Tea

Cross out each answer in the teapot as you solve the problems.

a.

$$\begin{array}{r} 30 \\ -\ 16 \\ \hline \end{array}$$

b.

$$\begin{array}{r} 12 \\ -\ 11 \\ \hline \end{array}$$

c.

$$\begin{array}{r} 32 \\ -\ 25 \\ \hline \end{array}$$

d.

$$\begin{array}{r} 50 \\ -\ 36 \\ \hline \end{array}$$

e.

$$\begin{array}{r} 79 \\ -\ 49 \\ \hline \end{array}$$

f.

$$\begin{array}{r} 91 \\ -\ 50 \\ \hline \end{array}$$

g.

$$\begin{array}{r} 88 \\ -\ 62 \\ \hline \end{array}$$

h.

$$\begin{array}{r} 73 \\ -\ 43 \\ \hline \end{array}$$

i.

$$\begin{array}{r} 86 \\ -\ 26 \\ \hline \end{array}$$

j.

$$\begin{array}{r} 93 \\ -\ 52 \\ \hline \end{array}$$

14   1   30

41   7   26   41

60   14   30

Word Problems

Read each word problem. Write the number sentence it shows. Find the difference.

a	b

Farmer Cole raised 93 bushels of wheat. Farmer Dale raised 68 bushels. What is the difference in the number of bushels each raised?	Dennis scored 43 points in his basketball game. Claire scored 40. What is the difference in points each earned?

c	d

Jason bought a pair of shoes for 53 dollars. Clark bought a pair for 28 dollars. What is the difference paid?	Jill counted 83 ants near an ant hill. Jack counted 62. What is the difference in the ants counted?

Subtraction Solutions

Fill in the puzzle by solving the subtraction problems. Use the word names in the Word List.

Word List				
eleven	thirteen	fifteen	seventeen	nineteen
twelve	fourteen	sixteen	eighteen	twenty

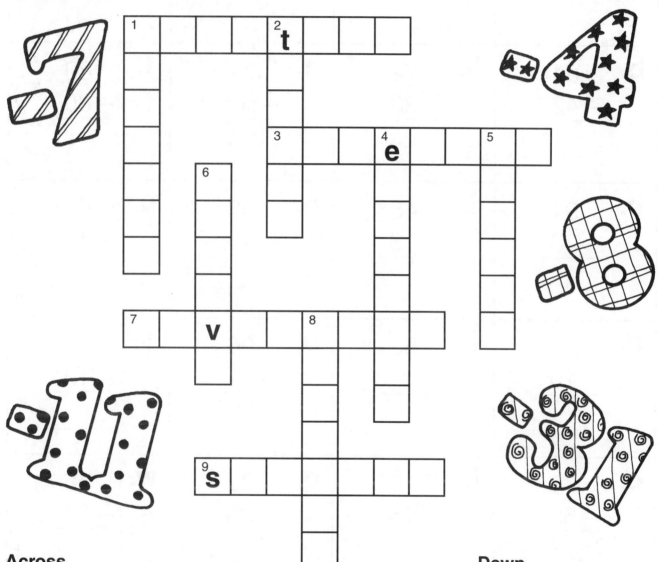

Across

1. 25 − 11 =
3. 40 − 21 =
7. 33 − 16 =
9. 51 − 35 =

Down

1. 46 − 31 =
2. 27 − 7 =
4. 22 − 4 =
5. 19 − 8 =
6. 44 − 32 =
8. 38 − 25 =

What's the Difference?

Find the differences.

a. $\begin{array}{r} 51 \\ -\ 50 \\ \hline \end{array}$	**g.** $\begin{array}{r} 69 \\ -\ 12 \\ \hline \end{array}$	**m.** $\begin{array}{r} 69 \\ -\ 16 \\ \hline \end{array}$	**s.** $\begin{array}{r} 36 \\ -\ 13 \\ \hline \end{array}$
b. $\begin{array}{r} 64 \\ -\ 42 \\ \hline \end{array}$	**h.** $\begin{array}{r} 72 \\ -\ 38 \\ \hline \end{array}$	**n.** $\begin{array}{r} 71 \\ -\ 59 \\ \hline \end{array}$	**t.** $\begin{array}{r} 89 \\ -\ 80 \\ \hline \end{array}$
c. $\begin{array}{r} 94 \\ -\ 23 \\ \hline \end{array}$	**i.** $\begin{array}{r} 48 \\ -\ 18 \\ \hline \end{array}$	**o.** $\begin{array}{r} 68 \\ -\ 13 \\ \hline \end{array}$	**u.** $\begin{array}{r} 51 \\ -\ 17 \\ \hline \end{array}$
d. $\begin{array}{r} 27 \\ -\ 10 \\ \hline \end{array}$	**j.** $\begin{array}{r} 52 \\ -\ 11 \\ \hline \end{array}$	**p.** $\begin{array}{r} 96 \\ -\ 41 \\ \hline \end{array}$	**v.** $\begin{array}{r} 91 \\ -\ 19 \\ \hline \end{array}$
e. $\begin{array}{r} 78 \\ -\ 52 \\ \hline \end{array}$	**k.** $\begin{array}{r} 19 \\ -\ 15 \\ \hline \end{array}$	**q.** $\begin{array}{r} 82 \\ -\ 30 \\ \hline \end{array}$	**w.** $\begin{array}{r} 46 \\ -\ 31 \\ \hline \end{array}$
f. $\begin{array}{r} 67 \\ -\ 14 \\ \hline \end{array}$	**l.** $\begin{array}{r} 62 \\ -\ 31 \\ \hline \end{array}$	**r.** $\begin{array}{r} 93 \\ -\ 90 \\ \hline \end{array}$	**x.** $\begin{array}{r} 87 \\ -\ 43 \\ \hline \end{array}$

Find the Difference

Find the differences.

a. $\begin{array}{r} 31 \\ -23 \\ \hline \end{array}$	**g.** $\begin{array}{r} 79 \\ -32 \\ \hline \end{array}$	**m.** $\begin{array}{r} 85 \\ -21 \\ \hline \end{array}$	**s.** $\begin{array}{r} 69 \\ -37 \\ \hline \end{array}$
b. $\begin{array}{r} 75 \\ -42 \\ \hline \end{array}$	**h.** $\begin{array}{r} 57 \\ -51 \\ \hline \end{array}$	**n.** $\begin{array}{r} 51 \\ -20 \\ \hline \end{array}$	**t.** $\begin{array}{r} 98 \\ -34 \\ \hline \end{array}$
c. $\begin{array}{r} 54 \\ -23 \\ \hline \end{array}$	**i.** $\begin{array}{r} 88 \\ -44 \\ \hline \end{array}$	**o.** $\begin{array}{r} 42 \\ -28 \\ \hline \end{array}$	**u.** $\begin{array}{r} 87 \\ -28 \\ \hline \end{array}$
d. $\begin{array}{r} 42 \\ -26 \\ \hline \end{array}$	**j.** $\begin{array}{r} 63 \\ -23 \\ \hline \end{array}$	**p.** $\begin{array}{r} 71 \\ -56 \\ \hline \end{array}$	**v.** $\begin{array}{r} 69 \\ -43 \\ \hline \end{array}$
e. $\begin{array}{r} 88 \\ -26 \\ \hline \end{array}$	**k.** $\begin{array}{r} 86 \\ -14 \\ \hline \end{array}$	**q.** $\begin{array}{r} 36 \\ -32 \\ \hline \end{array}$	**w.** $\begin{array}{r} 46 \\ -41 \\ \hline \end{array}$
f. $\begin{array}{r} 61 \\ -33 \\ \hline \end{array}$	**l.** $\begin{array}{r} 53 \\ -32 \\ \hline \end{array}$	**r.** $\begin{array}{r} 97 \\ -60 \\ \hline \end{array}$	**x.** $\begin{array}{r} 77 \\ -63 \\ \hline \end{array}$

What's the Scoop?

Fill in the missing number on each cone to complete the problem.

1.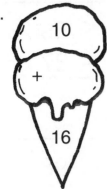
10
+
16

2.
17
− 8

3.
+ 4
17

4.
9
+
19

5.
8
−
1

6.
15
+ 4

7.
− 11
7

8.
21
− 16

9.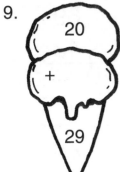
20
+
29

10.
14
− 7

11.
− 13
10

12.
14
+
25

13.
14
− 6

14.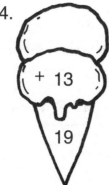
+ 13
19

15.
12
+ 12

16.
18
− 6

Sign In

Place + and − signs between the digits so that both sides of each equation are equal.

1.	6	4	1	2	6	2	=	15

2.	9	1	3	1	4	1	=	5

3.	9	3	4	1	2	3	=	14

4.	5	1	1	3	4	6	=	18

5.	9	8	6	3	5	3	=	8

6.	2	1	8	9	3	5	=	20

7.	5	3	2	4	1	5	=	12

8.	4	9	3	7	3	1	=	11

9.	7	6	2	8	7	1	=	3

10.	9	9	9	2	2	8	=	1

Times Tables

Complete the times tables.

0 x 0 = _____	1 x 6 = _____	2 x 12 = _____	4 x 5 = _____
0 x 1 = _____	1 x 7 = _____	3 x 0 = _____	4 x 6 = _____
0 x 2 = _____	1 x 8 = _____	3 x 1 = _____	4 x 7 = _____
0 x 3 = _____	1 x 9 = _____	3 x 2 = _____	4 x 8 = _____
0 x 4 = _____	1 x 10 = _____	3 x 3 = _____	4 x 9 = _____
0 x 5 = _____	1 x 11 = _____	3 x 4 = _____	4 x 10 = _____
0 x 6 = _____	1 x 12 = _____	3 x 5 = _____	4 x 11 = _____
0 x 7 = _____	2 x 0 = _____	3 x 6 = _____	4 x 12 = _____
0 x 8 = _____	2 x 1 = _____	3 x 7 = _____	5 x 0 = _____
0 x 9 = _____	2 x 2 = _____	3 x 8 = _____	5 x 1 = _____
0 x 10 = _____	2 x 3 = _____	3 x 9 = _____	5 x 2 = _____
0 x 11 = _____	2 x 4 = _____	3 x 10 = _____	5 x 3 = _____
0 x 12 = _____	2 x 5 = _____	3 x 11 = _____	5 x 4 = _____
1 x 0 = _____	2 x 6 = _____	3 x 12 = _____	5 x 5 = _____
1 x 1 = _____	2 x 7 = _____	4 x 0 = _____	5 x 6 = _____
1 x 2 = _____	2 x 8 = _____	4 x 1 = _____	5 x 7 = _____
1 x 3 = _____	2 x 9 = _____	4 x 2 = _____	5 x 8 = _____
1 x 4 = _____	2 x 10 = _____	4 x 3 = _____	5 x 9 = _____
1 x 5 = _____	2 x 11 = _____	4 x 4 = _____	5 x 10 = _____

Times Tables (cont.)

Complete the times tables.

5 x 11 = ____	7 x 4 = ____	8 x 10 = ____	10 x 3 = ____	11 x 9 = ____
5 x 12 = ____	7 x 5 = ____	8 x 11 = ____	10 x 4 = ____	11 x 10 = ____
6 x 0 = ____	7 x 6 = ____	8 x 12 = ____	10 x 5 = ____	11 x 11 = ____
6 x 1 = ____	7 x 7 = ____	9 x 0 = ____	10 x 6 = ____	11 x 12 = ____
6 x 2 = ____	7 x 8 = ____	9 x 1 = ____	10 x 7 = ____	12 x 0 = ____
6 x 3 = ____	7 x 9 = ____	9 x 2 = ____	10 x 8 = ____	12 x 1 = ____
6 x 4 = ____	7 x 10 = ____	9 x 3 = ____	10 x 9 = ____	12 x 2 = ____
6 x 5 = ____	7 x 11 = ____	9 x 4 = ____	10 x 10 = ____	12 x 3 = ____
6 x 6 = ____	7 x 12 = ____	9 x 5 = ____	10 x 11 = ____	12 x 4 = ____
6 x 7 = ____	8 x 0 = ____	9 x 6 = ____	10 x 12 = ____	12 x 5 = ____
6 x 8 = ____	8 x 1 = ____	9 x 7 = ____	11 x 0 = ____	12 x 6 = ____
6 x 9 = ____	8 x 2 = ____	9 x 8 = ____	11 x 1 = ____	12 x 7 = ____
6 x 10 = ____	8 x 3 = ____	9 x 9 = ____	11 x 2 = ____	12 x 8 = ____
6 x 11 = ____	8 x 4 = ____	9 x 10 = ____	11 x 3 = ____	12 x 9 = ____
6 x 12 = ____	8 x 5 = ____	9 x 11 = ____	11 x 4 = ____	12 x 10 = ____
7 x 0 = ____	8 x 6 = ____	9 x 12 = ____	11 x 5 = ____	12 x 11 = ____
7 x 1 = ____	8 x 7 = ____	10 x 0 = ____	11 x 6 = ____	12 x 12 = ____
7 x 2 = ____	8 x 8 = ____	10 x 1 = ____	11 x 7 = ____	
7 x 3 = ____	8 x 9 = ____	10 x 2 = ____	11 x 8 = ____	

Multiplication

Solve the problems.

2 x 2	12 x 5	6 x 1	6 x 3
3 x 8	7 x 5	7 x 7	7 x 9
5 x 1	11 x 8	9 x 0	9 x 2
10 x 0	10 x 4	10 x 6	10 x 8
2 x 3	11 x 10	11 x 12	12 x 1
11 x 5	6 x 0	6 x 2	6 x 4
7 x 4	7 x 6	7 x 8	10 x 7
10 x 8	12 x 8	9 x 1	9 x 3
10 x 3	10 x 5	10 x 7	10 x 9
11 x 9	11 x 11	12 x 0	12 x 2

Column Multiplication

Solve the problems.

96 x 16	68 x 88	56 x 75	22 x 67
90 x 13	33 x 31	84 x 28	74 x 17
47 x 19	20 x 62	70 x 96	26 x 93
25 x 11	24 x 19	58 x 75	14 x 72
26 x 16	41 x 40	50 x10	48 x 30
40 x 28	46 x 20	21 x 25	42 x 48
82 x 35	49 x 71	77 x 63	88 x 50
60 x 52	38 x 45	79 x 44	69 x 18
71 x 27	24 x 35	86 x 33	43 x 31
32 x 54	27 x 32	13 x 29	19 x 22

By Three

Solve the problems.

173 x 6	533 x 8	138 x 2	833 x 5
227 x 3	388 x 1	417 x 8	524 x 3
402 x 1	620 x 6	317 x 4	468 x 6
420 x 8	662 x 3	458 x 7	947 x 2
178 x 9	714 x 9	550 x 6	767 x 7
324 x 8	835 x 3	594 x 5	632 x 3
172 x 4	152 x 7	180 x 4	221 x 2
286 x 8	254 x 5	538 x 1	489 x 4
509 x 4	851 x 1	728 x 6	141 x 9
615 x 2	674 x 8	107 x 3	213 x 5

Double Time

Solve the problems.

23 x 16	13 x 38	89 x 57	44 x 76
90 x 39	31 x 11	24 x 23	22 x 51
17 x 79	41 x 96	74 x 19	16 x 39
35 x 15	14 x 79	48 x 79	25 x 17
14 x 63	80 x 54	70 x 71	28 x 93
56 x 82	34 x 24	21 x 26	58 x 48
73 x 50	46 x 27	67 x 64	99 x 56
50 x 28	68 x 40	39 x 42	64 x 48
81 x 76	34 x 83	96 x 30	34 x 23
51 x 44	23 x 36	18 x 28	36 x 20

Division Facts

Solve the problems.

0 ÷ 0 = _____	6 ÷ 1 = _____	24 ÷ 12 = _____	24 ÷ 4 = _____
1 ÷ 0 = _____	7 ÷ 1 = _____	3 ÷ 3 = _____	28 ÷ 4 = _____
2 ÷ 0 = _____	8 ÷ 1 = _____	6 ÷ 3 = _____	32 ÷ 4 = _____
3 ÷ 0 = _____	9 ÷ 1 = _____	9 ÷ 3 = _____	36 ÷ 4 = _____
4 ÷ 0 = _____	10 ÷ 1 = _____	12 ÷ 3 = _____	40 ÷ 4 = _____
5 ÷ 0 = _____	11 ÷ 1 = _____	15 ÷ 3 = _____	44 ÷ 4 = _____
6 ÷ 0 = _____	12 ÷ 1 = _____	18 ÷ 3 = _____	48 ÷ 4 = _____
7 ÷ 0 = _____	2 ÷ 2 = _____	21 ÷ 3 = _____	5 ÷ 5 = _____
8 ÷ 0 = _____	4 ÷ 2 = _____	24 ÷ 3 = _____	10 ÷ 5 = _____
9 ÷ 0 = _____	6 ÷ 2 = _____	27 ÷ 3 = _____	15 ÷ 5 = _____
10 ÷ 0 = _____	8 ÷ 2 = _____	30 ÷ 3 = _____	20 ÷ 5 = _____
11 ÷ 0 = _____	10 ÷ 2 = _____	33 ÷ 3 = _____	25 ÷ 5 = _____
12 ÷ 0 = _____	12 ÷ 2 = _____	36 ÷ 3 = _____	30 ÷ 5 = _____
1 ÷ 1 = _____	14 ÷ 2 = _____	4 ÷ 4 = _____	35 ÷ 5 = _____
2 ÷ 1 = _____	16 ÷ 2 = _____	8 ÷ 4 = _____	40 ÷ 5 = _____
3 ÷ 1 = _____	18 ÷ 2 = _____	12 ÷ 4 = _____	45 ÷ 5 = _____
4 ÷ 1 = _____	20 ÷ 2 = _____	16 ÷ 4 = _____	50 ÷ 5 = _____
5 ÷ 1 = _____	22 ÷ 2 = _____	20 ÷ 4 = _____	55 ÷ 5 = _____

© *Teacher Created Materials, Inc.*

Division Facts (cont.)

Solve the problems.

$60 \div 5 =$ ___	$42 \div 7 =$ ___	$96 \div 8 =$ ___	$60 \div 10 =$ ___	$132 \div 11 =$ ___
$6 \div 6 =$ ___	$49 \div 7 =$ ___	$9 \div 9 =$ ___	$70 \div 10 =$ ___	$12 \div 12 =$ ___
$12 \div 6 =$ ___	$56 \div 7 =$ ___	$18 \div 9 =$ ___	$80 \div 10 =$ ___	$24 \div 12 =$ ___
$18 \div 6 =$ ___	$63 \div 7 =$ ___	$27 \div 9 =$ ___	$90 \div 10 =$ ___	$36 \div 12 =$ ___
$24 \div 6 =$ ___	$70 \div 7 =$ ___	$36 \div 9 =$ ___	$100 \div 10 =$ ___	$48 \div 12 =$ ___
$30 \div 6 =$ ___	$77 \div 7 =$ ___	$45 \div 9 =$ ___	$110 \div 10 =$ ___	$60 \div 12 =$ ___
$36 \div 6 =$ ___	$84 \div 7 =$ ___	$54 \div 9 =$ ___	$120 \div 10 =$ ___	$72 \div 12 =$ ___
$42 \div 6 =$ ___	$8 \div 8 =$ ___	$63 \div 9 =$ ___	$11 \div 11 =$ ___	$84 \div 12 =$ ___
$48 \div 6 =$ ___	$16 \div 8 =$ ___	$72 \div 9 =$ ___	$22 \div 11 =$ ___	$96 \div 12 =$ ___
$54 \div 6 =$ ___	$24 \div 8 =$ ___	$81 \div 9 =$ ___	$33 \div 11 =$ ___	$108 \div 12 =$ ___
$60 \div 6 =$ ___	$32 \div 8 =$ ___	$90 \div 9 =$ ___	$44 \div 11 =$ ___	$120 \div 12 =$ ___
$66 \div 6 =$ ___	$40 \div 8 =$ ___	$99 \div 9 =$ ___	$55 \div 11 =$ ___	$132 \div 12 =$ ___
$72 \div 6 =$ ___	$48 \div 8 =$ ___	$108 \div 9 =$ ___	$66 \div 11 =$ ___	$144 \div 12 =$ ___
$7 \div 7 =$ ___	$56 \div 8 =$ ___	$10 \div 10 =$ ___	$77 \div 11 =$ ___	
$14 \div 7 =$ ___	$64 \div 8 =$ ___	$20 \div 10 =$ ___	$88 \div 11 =$ ___	
$21 \div 7 =$ ___	$72 \div 8 =$ ___	$30 \div 10 =$ ___	$99 \div 11 =$ ___	
$28 \div 7 =$ ___	$80 \div 8 =$ ___	$40 \div 10 =$ ___	$110 \div 11 =$ ___	
$35 \div 7 =$ ___	$88 \div 8 =$ ___	$50 \div 10 =$ ___	$121 \div 11 =$ ___	

Divide and Conquer

Solve the problems.

16)400   15)225   18)234

12)240   10)180   8)136

5)95   8)248   2)112

16)256   6)150   32)128

16)288   9)171   11)231

Which Is It?

Read the number sentences. Add the correct math sign to each problem.

+	−	x	÷
add	subtract	multiply	divide

1. 5 _____ 7 = 12

2. 24 _____ 4 = 6

3. 9 _____ 3 = 12

4. 18 _____ 6 = 12

5. 4 _____ 9 = 13

6. 4 _____ 9 = 36

7. 10 _____ 8 = 80

8. 15 _____ 5 = 3

9. 11 _____ 4 = 7

10. 8 _____ 16 = 24

11. 2 _____ 8 = 16

12. 3 _____ 2 = 5

13. 22 _____ 6 = 16

14. 9 _____ 1 = 10

15. 3 _____ 3 = 9

16. 144 _____ 12 = 12

17. 21 _____ 3 = 7

18. 90 _____ 10 = 9

19. 12 _____ 11 = 132

20. 14 _____ 1 = 14

Picture Fractions

A **fraction** is a number that names part of a whole thing. The number at the top is the numerator. It tells how many parts of the whole are present. The number at the bottom is the denominator. It tells how many parts there are in all.

Examples

 $\frac{1}{2}$ (There are two parts in the circle. One part is gray. Therefore, the fraction is $\frac{1}{2}$.)

 $\frac{3}{4}$ (There are four parts in the square. Three parts are gray. The fraction is $\frac{3}{4}$.)

Write a fraction for each picture.

1. 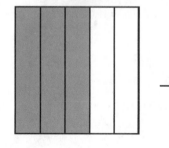 _____

2. 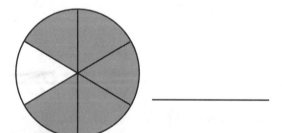 _____

3. 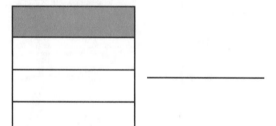 _____

4.  _____

5. 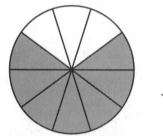 _____

6. 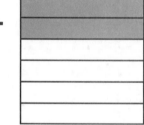 _____

7. 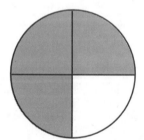 _____

8. 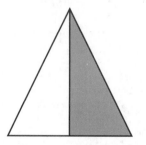 _____

Slice It Up!

In a **circle graph**, all the parts must add up to be a whole. Think of the parts like pieces that add up to one whole pie. Look at these pies and how they are divided into pieces.

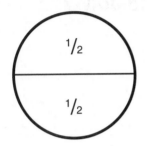

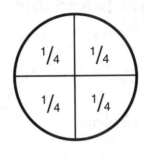

1/2 a pie

+ 1/2 a pie

2 halves =

1 whole pie

1/4 a pie

+ 1/4 a pie

+ 1/4 a pie

+ 1/4 a pie

4 fourths =

1 whole pie

Make a circle graph to show how much pie a family ate. Here is the information you will need.

Mother ate 1/4 of the pie.

Sister ate 1/4 of the pie.

Father ate 1/4 of the pie.

Brother ate 1/8 of the pie.

Grandma ate 1/8 of the pie.

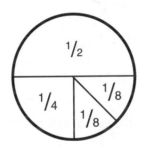

1/8 a pie

+ 1/8 a pie

+ 1/8 a pie

+ 1/8 a pie

+ 1/8 a pie

+ 1/8 a pie

+ 1/8 a pie

+ 1/8 a pie

8 eighths =

1 whole pie

1/2 a pie = 1 half

+ 1/4 a pie = 1 fourth

+ 1/8 a pie = 1 eighth

+ 1/8 a pie = 1 eighth

1 whole pie

Color the graph below using the Color Key.

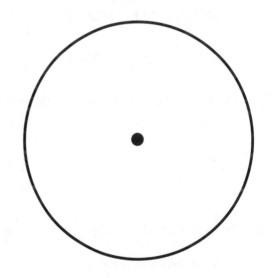

Pie My Family Ate

Color Key

sister = orange   mother = pink

grandma = red   brother = yellow

father = blue

Circle Graph

Shown in this circle graph are the types of fruit sold at a produce stand in a week in July.

Fruits Sold at O'Henry's Fruit Stand July 1 to July 7

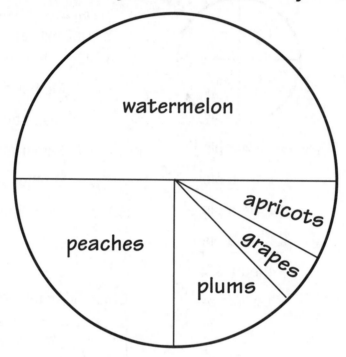

1. What fruit sold the most at O'Henry's Fruit Stand? _____

2. What fruit sold the least? _____

3. Rank the order of the fruits that were sold. Number 1 will be the fruit that sold most, number 5, least.

   1. _____ 2. _____ 3. _____

   4. _____ 5. _____

4. Circle the correct fraction.

   Watermelon was   1/2   1/4   1/8   of all the fruit sold.

   Peaches were   1/2   1/4   1/8   of all the fruit sold.

   Plums were   1/2   1/4   1/8   of all the fruit sold.

5. Which of the fruits represented on the circle graph is your favorite?

   _____

Slices

Look at this circle graph. It shows what Chris did during one hour of time at home.

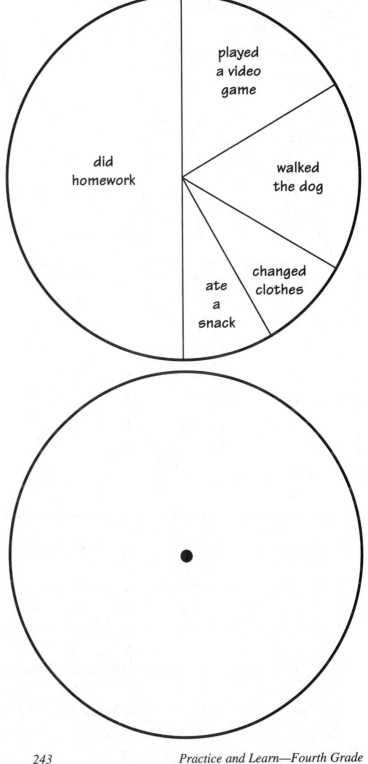

What Chris did from 4 to 5 P.M. on November 5

1. How many minutes did Chris spend . . .

    doing homework? _____

    eating a snack? _____

    changing clothes? _____

    playing a video game? _____

    walking the dog? _____

2. How did you figure out the number of minutes Chris did things?

    _____

    _____

Make a circle graph that shows what you did during one of your after-school hours.

Write the title of your graph here.

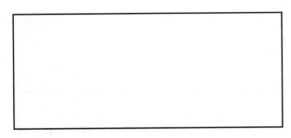

At the Playground

Using metric measurement, answer the questions below the playground map. Give all of your answers in meters. Draw lines between the areas and measure between the dots.

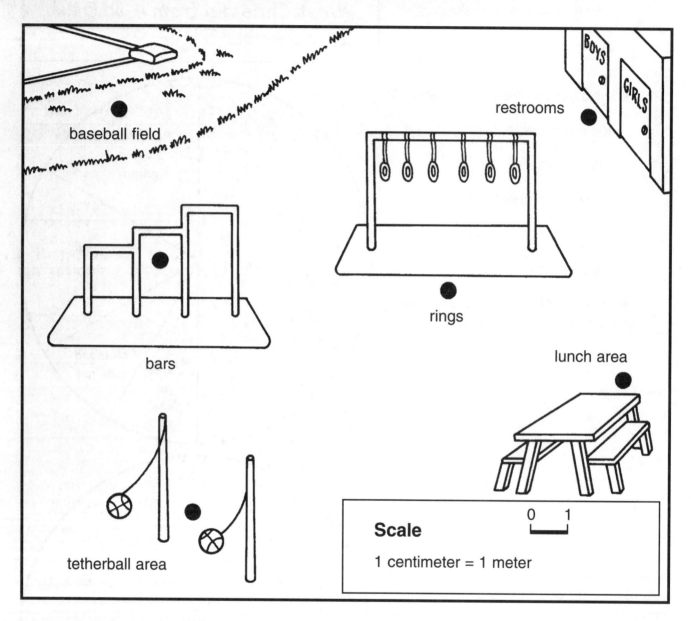

1. About how far is it from the bars to the baseball field? _____

2. About how far is it from the rings to the tetherball area? _____

3. About how far is it from the restrooms to the bars? _____

4. About how far is it from the lunch area to the bars? _____

5. About how far is it from the baseball field to the lunch area? _____

Measurement Choices

Measurement for a map scale can be given in inches, feet, and miles. This type of measurement is called **standard measure**.

Measurement for a map scale can also be given in centimeters, meters, and kilometers. This type of measurement is called **metric measure**.

On some map scales, both standard and metric measure are used. It is good to learn how to read and use both kinds of measurement systems.

When we choose a scale to use, it needs to be suited to the type of map we are making.

What do you think?

Decide on an appropriate scale to measure the size or distance of each of the following things. Use the scales in the box as your choices. Be ready to explain your choices.

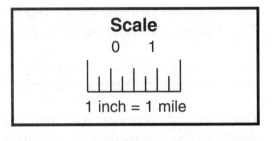

Scale

1 inch = 1 mile

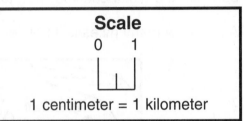

Scale

1 centimeter = 1 kilometer

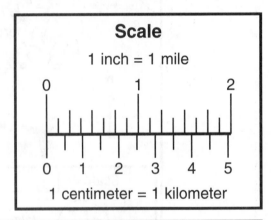

Scale

1 inch = 1 mile

1 centimeter = 1 kilometer

a. 1 centimeter = 1 centimeter	d. 1 inch = 1 foot
b. 1 centimeter = 1 meter	e. 1 inch = 1 mile
c. 1 centimeter = 1 kilometer	f. 1 inch = 100 miles

1. A cricket _____

2. Oregon to Texas _____

3. A bicycle race course _____

4. Your bedroom _____

5. Length of a sofa _____

6. Length of a horse's body _____

7. A swimming pool _____

8. The Mississippi River _____

9. The town park to your house _____

10. Your toes _____

How to Measure

When you measure distances using a map scale, you can measure several different ways. The easiest and most accurate way is to use a standard measure or metric measure ruler.

You can also use a piece of string, paper, the joints of your fingers, a pencil or pen, or other things that could help you mark size.

Once you have chosen your measurement instrument, place it along the imaginary or real line between the distances you want to measure.

About how many miles is it between:

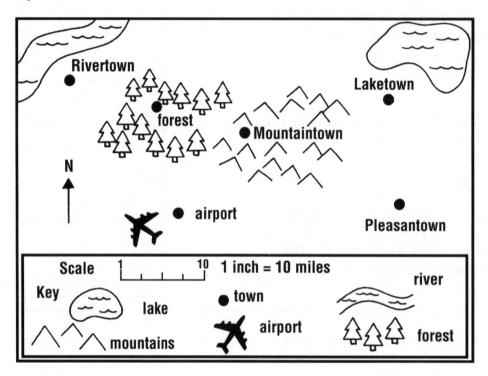

1. Rivertown and the airport? _____

2. Mountaintown and the forest? _____

3. Rivertown and Laketown? _____

4. Mountaintown and Pleasantown? _____

5. Laketown and Mountaintown? _____

6. Rivertown and the forest? _____

Is it farther from Pleasantown to Laketown or from Pleasantown to Mountaintown?

_____

From Here to There

Use this map scale and a metric ruler to answer the distance questions on this page. Use the center of the dots to measure.

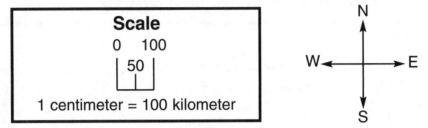

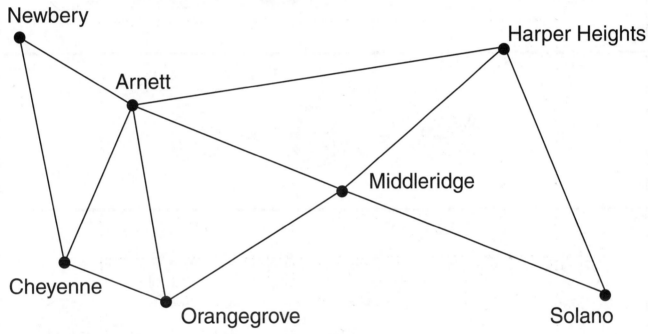

1. Newbery is _____ kilometers from Solano.

2. Middleridge is _____ kilometers from Orangegrove.

3. Cheyenne is _____ kilometers from Arnett.

4. Orangegrove is _____ kilometers from Harper Heights.

5. Arnett is _____ kilometers from Solano.

6. Harper Heights is _____ kilometers from Arnett.

7. Solano is _____ kilometers from Middleridge.

8. Middleridge is _____ kilometers from Harper Heights.

9. Newbery is _____ kilometers from Cheyenne.

10. Arnett is _____ kilometers from Middleridge.

How Much Is It Worth?

Read this money chart. Then answer the questions below.

Pennies, Nickels, and Dimes

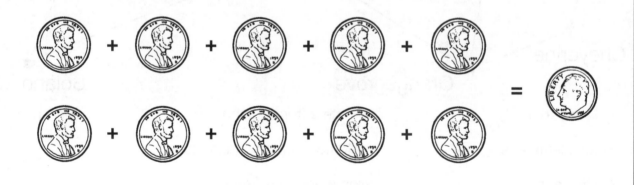

1. A penny is worth _____.

2. A nickel is worth _____.

3. A dime is worth _____.

4. _____ pennies equal _____ nickel.

5. _____ nickels equal _____ dime.

6. _____ pennies equal _____ dime.

7. 5 pennies equal _____.

8. 2 nickels equal _____.

9. 10 pennies equal _____.

10. 1 dime, 1 nickel, and 1 penny equal _____.

Change, Please

List the coins you would give each person below to make change for his or her dollar.

1. Dolly wants 1 coin for her $1. _____

2. Zac wants 6 coins for his $1. _____

3. Holly wants 7 coins for her $1. _____

4. Andrew wants 10 coins for his $1. _____

5. Casie wants 15 coins for her $1. _____

6. Thomas wants 16 coins for his $1. _____

7. Chelsea wants 17 coins for her $1. _____

8. Austin wants 19 coins for his $1. _____

9. Marc wants 25 coins for his $1. _____

10. Roberto wants 28 coins for his $1. _____

Change for Fifty Cents

There are over 75 ways to make change for 50 cents. Work with a friend to list as many ways as you can. List the coins in order on each line, from largest to smallest. (**Hint:** Working from large to small coins will also help you find more ways to make change.) The list has been started for you. If you need more space, continue your list on the back of this paper.

Use the following abbreviations:

hd (half dollar)   **q** (quarter)   **d** (dime)   **n** (nickel)   **p** (penny)

1. 1 hd	11.
2. 2 q	12.
3.	13.
4.	14.
5.	15.
6.	16.
7.	17.
8.	18.
9.	19.
10.	20.

Change for a Dollar

There are over 200 ways to make change for a dollar. Work with a friend to list as many ways as you can. List the coins in order on each line, from largest to smallest. (*Hint:* Working from large to small coins will help you find more ways to make change, too.) The list has been started for you. If you need more space, continue your list on the back of this paper.

Use the following abbreviations:

hd *(half dollar)*   **q** *(quarter)*   **d** *(dime)*   **n** *(nickel)*   **p** *(penny)*

1. 2hd
2. 1hd and 2q
3. 1hd and 5d
4. 1hd and 10n
5. _____
6. _____
7. _____
8. _____
9. _____
10. _____
11. _____
12. _____
13. _____
14. _____
15. _____
16. _____
17. _____
18. _____
19. _____
20. _____
21. _____
22. _____
23. _____
24. _____
25. _____

26. _____
27. _____
28. _____
29. _____
30. _____
31. _____
32. _____
33. _____
34. _____
35. _____
36. _____
37. _____
38. _____
39. _____
40. _____
41. _____
42. _____
43. _____
44. _____
45. _____
46. _____
47. _____
48. _____
49. _____
50. _____

A.M. and P.M.

A.M. is the time after 12 o'clock midnight and before 12 o'clock noon. **P.M.** is the time after 12 o'clock noon and before 12 o'clock midnight. (Midnight itself is A.M. and noon itself is P.M.) Write **A.M.** or **P.M.** after each of these events to say what time it usually falls in.

1. dinner time _____

2. getting up _____

3. afternoon nap _____

4. after-school baseball game _____

5. before-school dance class _____

6. breakfast _____

7. evening movie _____

8. evening bath _____

9. after-dinner dessert _____

10. sunrise _____

11. going to school _____

12. sunset _____

13. lunch _____

14. morning cartoons _____

15. going to bed _____

16. after-school piano lessons _____

17. morning exercises _____

18. homework _____

19. afternoon reading _____

20. morning snack _____

Timely Chore

Each word in the time box refers to a specific time span. List the words in order from the shortest time span to the longest. Then, explain how long each time span is.

Time Span	**How Long Is It?**
1. _____	_____
2. _____	_____
3. _____	_____
4. _____	_____
5. _____	_____
6. _____	_____
7. _____	_____
8. _____	_____
9. _____	_____
10. _____	_____
11. _____	_____
12. _____	_____

Time Box

second	hour	millennium
fortnight	day	month
minute	score	century
year	decade	week

Exam Time

As Mr. Teran prepared to pass back the last spelling exam, five anxious students awaited their grades. Using the clues below, determine each child's grade. Mark an **X** in each correct box.

1. Lucy, who did not get an A on her test, scored higher than Martin and Gwen.

2. Cara and Gwen both scored higher than Donald.

3. Martin received a C on his test.

4. No two students received the same grade.

	A	B	C	C-	D
Lucy					
Gwen					
Cara					
Martin					
Donald					

Theodore

Mr. Martin has three boys in his science class who each go by a variation of the name Theodore. From the statements below, discover each boy's full name and age. Mark the correct boxes with an **X**.

1. Agee is younger than Dalton but older than Chin.

2. Ted is not the youngest or the oldest.

3. Theodore's last name is Chin.

4. None of the boys is the same age.

	Agee	Chin	Dalton	8	9	10
Ted						
Theodore						
Teddy						

© Teacher Created Materials, Inc.

Favorite Teams

Five boys root for five different baseball teams. Read the clues to determine which team each likes best. Mark the correct boxes with an **X**.

1. Will's bedroom is filled with posters and products from the A's.

2. Andrew's father is a big Cardinals fan, but Andrew is not.

3. Chad and Ryan like the Dodgers, the Reds, or the A's.

4. No boy's favorite team begins with the same letter as his name.

	Cardinals	Dodgers	A's	Reds	White Sox
Chad					
Danny					
Andrew					
Ryan					
Will					

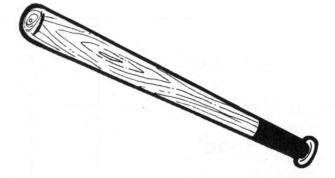

A Visit to the Amusement Park

Katelyn, Kenny, Emily, and Howie recently visited their local amusement park to ride their favorite attractions—the roller coaster, the Ferris wheel, the carousel, and the bumper cars. While there, one ate a hamburger, another ate a corndog, another ate a hot dog, and the last ate bratwurst. Using the clues below, determine each person's favorite ride plus what each had to eat. Mark the correct boxes with an **X**.

	roller coaster	Ferris wheel	carousel	bumper cars	hamburger	corndog	hot dog	bratwurst
Katelyn								
Kenny								
Emily								
Howie								

1. The girls liked the roller coaster and bumper cars while the boys liked the Ferris wheel and the carousel.

2. Howie ate his food on a stick while Katelyn ate hers on a hot dog bun.

3. Katelyn's favorite ride has hills.

4. The boy who loved the Ferris wheel also loves hot dogs.

Softball Lineup

All nine players on the Tiger softball team are sitting on the bench in their batting order. Using the clues below, find their batting order. Record their batting order by putting an **X** in the correct box.

1. Jane is batting fifth, and Daisy will bat some time before Carrie.

2. Joanne sits between Daisy and Gertie, and Annie is to the right of Jane.

3. Gertie bats after Joanne but before Annie.

4. Penny sits next to Carrie.

5. Carrie and Tammy are at each end of the bench.

	1	2	3	4	5	6	7	8	9
Jane									
Daisy									
Carrie									
Joanne									
Gertie									
Annie									
Penny									
Tammy									
Lindsey									

Intermediate Points

Study this compass rose.

You are familiar with the four cardinal points, but there are times when directions can not be given using simply north, south, east, or west.

You need to be able to show points that come between the four primary directions. Intermediate points give a mapmaker just such a tool.

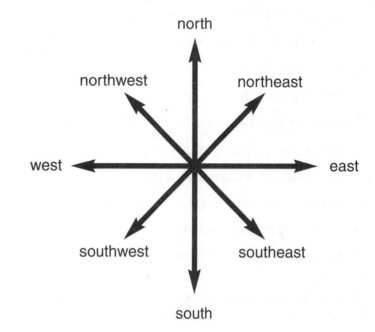

As you can see, the new direction words are made by combining the names of the cardinal points.

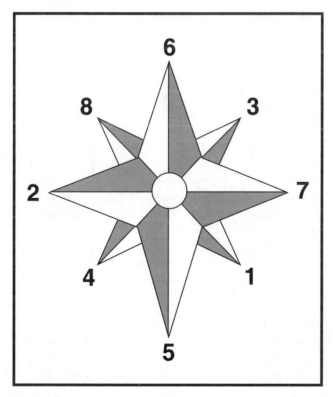

Using the cardinal and intermediate points, write the locations of the numbers in the box on the left.

1. _____

2. _____

3. _____

4. _____

5. _____

6. _____ **north** _____

7. _____

8. _____

Can You Find Home?

You are lost. Can you find your home by following the directions in the box below?

1. Begin in the most northwest home.
2. Move three houses east.
3. Move one house south.
4. Move two houses southwest.
5. Move one house west.
6. Move three houses northeast.
7. Move two houses southeast.
8. Move five houses west.
9. Move two houses north.
10. Move three houses southeast.

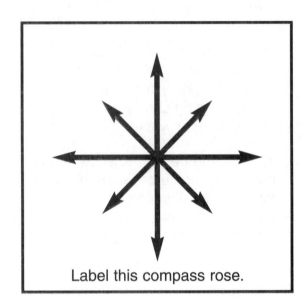

Label this compass rose.

Follow these directions. Color each of the houses you touch red. Color your home a different color.

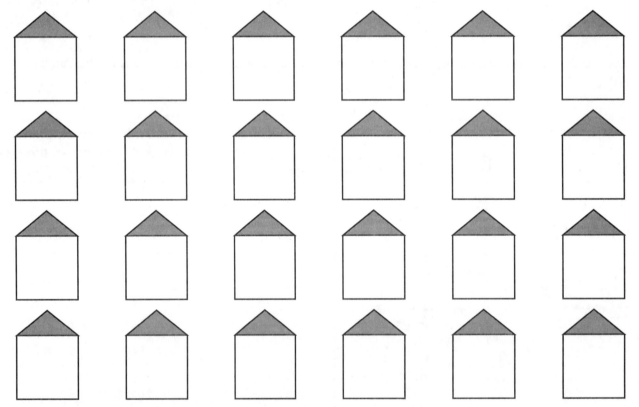

Can you rewrite the directions using fewer steps?

_____

_____

I've Got the Key!

Mapmakers draw the symbols they use in a map key. The map key explains what each symbol represents.

Look at this map and the map key. Use it to answer the questions below.

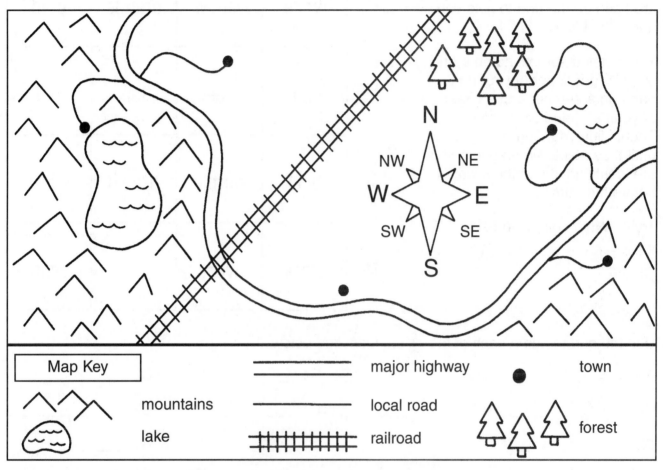

Answer true or false. If it is false, write the correct answer below it.

1. _____ A railroad track runs southwest to northeast.

2. _____ Mountains cover the northern section of the map.

3. _____ A lake and a forest are in the southeast.

4. _____ All towns can be reached by the major highway.

5. _____ Two towns are by lakes, and two towns are in the mountains.

6. _____ There are no towns along the railroad track.

7. _____ There is a large forest east of the lake and west of the railroad.

8. _____ The southernmost town is next to the major highway.

Grids

A **grid** is an arrangement of blocks that are made by vertical and horizontal lines intersecting on a page. Numbers and letters are used on the grid to help you name the blocks.

You can find something on a grid by putting a finger of your right hand on a number and a finger of your left hand on a letter. Then, slide your fingers together until they meet. When grid points are identified, the letter is written before the number.

Try it! What color is in block C4?

_____

	1	2	3	4
A	white	yellow	orange	gold
B	pink	green	tan	red
C	blue	purple	brown	silver
D	black	ivory	gray	lavender

Use the grid to name each of the colors identified below.

A1 _____	D3 _____	B4 _____	D2 _____
C4 _____	A2 _____	D1 _____	C2 _____
B3 _____	A4 _____	C3 _____	B1 _____
D4 _____	B2 _____	A3 _____	C1 _____

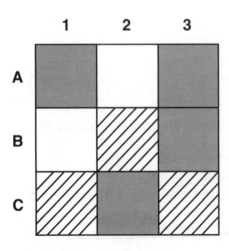

Use the grid on the left to answer these questions.

Which blocks are shaded?

_____

Which blocks are striped?

_____

Which blocks are unmarked?

_____

Where in This City?

Use the grid on the city map to find the places listed at the bottom of the page. Write the letter before the number for each place you find.

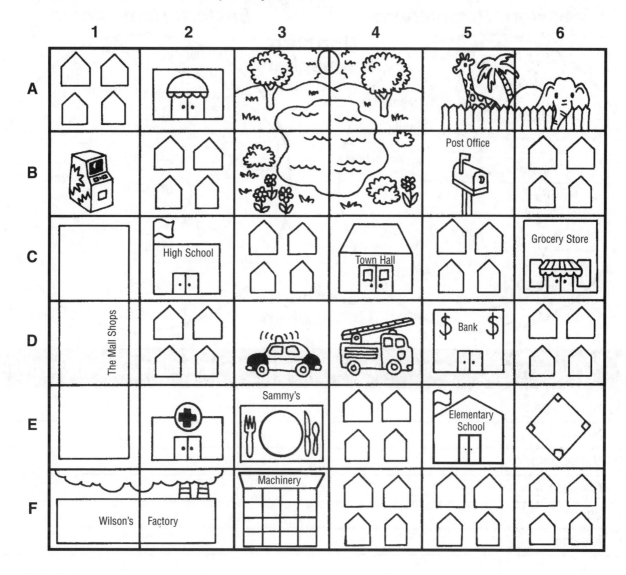

1. Medical Center _____
2. Machinery Warehouse _____
3. The Mall Shops _____, _____, and _____
4. Elementary School _____
5. Sammy's Restaurant _____
6. Green Park _____, _____, _____, and _____
7. Wilson's Factory _____, _____
8. City Zoo _____ and _____

9. City Bank _____
10. Town Hall _____
11. Ball Field _____
12. Arcade _____
13. Fire Station _____
14. Post Office _____
15. Grocery Store _____
16. High School _____

Where Is It?

Use the hemisphere maps on this page to help you locate the correct hemisphere for the places listed below.

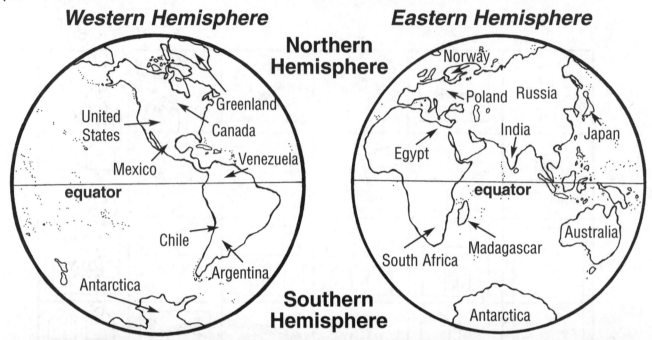

Place	Hemisphere (Northern or Southern)	Hemisphere (Eastern or Western)
1. South Africa		
2. Norway		
3. Venezuela		
4. Canada		
5. Japan		
6. Mexico		
7. Russia		
8. Egypt		
9. United States		
10. Argentina		
11. Poland		
12. Greenland		
13. India		
14. Chile		
15. Madagascar		
16. Australia		

How Many Degrees?

The intersection of Earth's latitude and longitude lines form a grid. All of these lines have degree markings. If you know the degrees of latitude and longitude of a certain place, you can easily find it on the map.

The map of Colorado below shows the latitude and longitude lines that divide the state. Use the map to answer these questions.

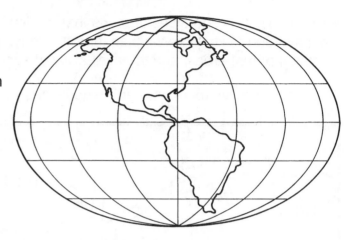

Which city is near . . .

1. 39 N, 109 W? _____

2. 41 N, 103 W? _____

3. 40 N, 105 W? _____

4. 38 N, 102 W? _____

5. 37 N, 108 W? _____

6. 39 N, 105 W? _____

7. 39 N, 107 W? _____

8. 37 N, 103 W? _____

9. 41 N, 108 W? _____

10. 39 N, 102 W? _____

109° W	108° W	107° W	106° W	105° W	104° W	103° W	102° W

41° N

Craig

Sterling

40° N

Glenwood Springs

★ **Denver**

Kanorado

39° N

Grand Junction

● Colorado Springs

COLORADO

Pueblo

Lamar

38° N

Durango

Trinidad

Campo

37° N

109° W	108° W	107° W	106° W	105° W	104° W	103° W	102° W

Road Maps

Road maps show the types of roads that are in a specific area. They also tell us other things we may need to know as we plan for travel, such as the distances from town to town, the locations of rest areas, and the availability of scenic routes.

After you read this map, answer the questions at the bottom of the page.

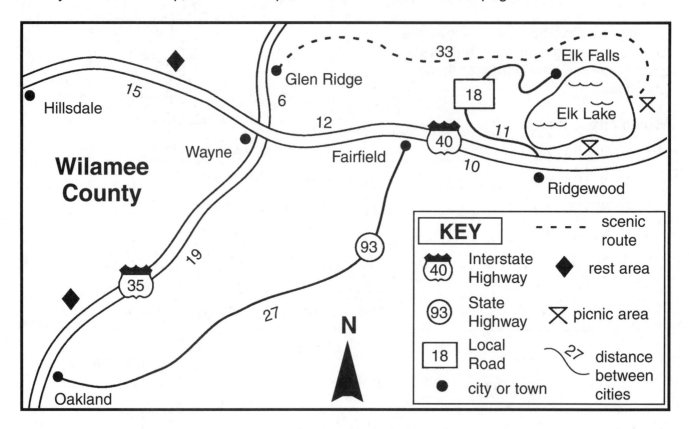

Distances Between Cities

1. Near what highways are the rest areas? _____

2. If you travel on State Highway 93, what is the distance from Oakland to Fairfield?

   _____

3. Interstate Highways 35 and 40 intersect at what city?_____

4. There is a scenic route that ends at the east side of Elk Lake. Where does it begin?

   _____

5. What is the distance from Hillsdale to:

   a. Wayne? _____   b. Ridgewood? _____

   c. Fairfield?_____   d. Elk Falls? _____

How Many Miles to Go?

Use the map on this page to answer the questions.

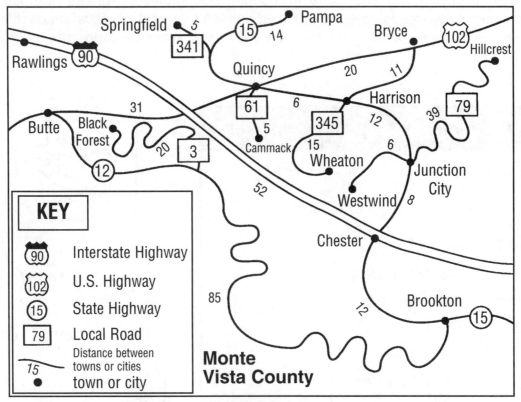

Distances Between Towns and Cities

1. You are in Butte. How far do you have to travel to

    a. Quincy? _____   b. Pampa? _____   c. Harrison? _____

    d. Hillcrest? _____   e. Bryce? _____   f. Brookton? _____

2. You are in Westwind. How far do you have to travel to

    a. Junction City? _____   b. Chester? _____   c. Bryce? _____

    d. Hillcrest? _____   e. Rawlings? _____   f. Cammack? _____

3. You are in Hillcrest. How far do you have to travel to

    a. Rawlings? _____   b. Bryce? _____   c. Wheaton? _____

    d. Brookton? _____   e. Westwind? _____   f. Pampa? _____

Challenge: Describe the route that would be fastest from Butte to Brookton.

_____

Why?_____

_____

Political Maps

One type of map that uses boundary lines is called a **political map**. A political map gives us information about county, province, state, and county boundaries as well as information about cities, towns, highways, roads, forest areas, and points of interest. Political maps also show oceans, rivers, and lakes, but they do not show the elevations of the land area as physical maps do.

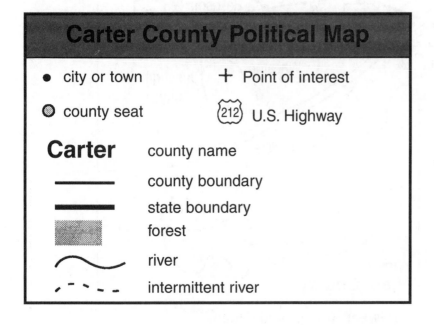

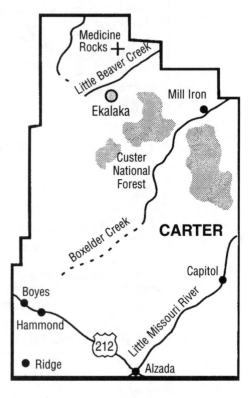

Use this political map of Carter County, Montana, to answer the questions below.

1. Which sides of Montana's border does Carter County help form? _____

   _____

2. What is the name of the county seat? _____

3. Through what three cities does the U.S. highway pass? _____

   _____

4. Name one intermittent river in Carter County. _____

5. What is the point of interest in this county? _____

On a separate piece of paper, make a political map of the county in which you live.

Historical Maps

There is another type of map that makes use of boundary lines. These maps are called **historical maps** and show something about the history of an area.

At the time of Columbus, there were about 300 Native American tribes in North America. These tribes are often divided into seven groups: Woodland, Plains, Southwestern, California-Intermountain, Pacific Coast, Far North, and Middle American.

Use this historical map to answer questions about the Native American of early North America.

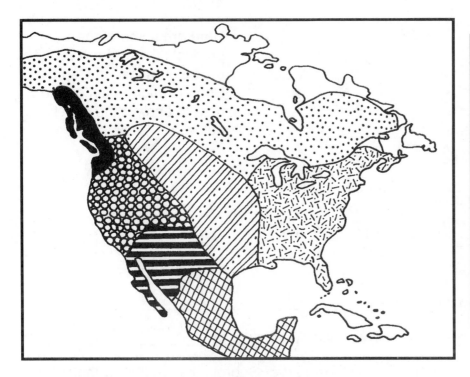

Native American Group Key

- Woodland
- Plains
- Southwestern
- California-Intermountain
- Pacific Coast
- Far North
- Middle American

1. What group of Native Americans covered the largest North American area?

   _____

2. What group of Native Americans were both in Mexico and the United States?

   _____

3. What group of Native Americans covered the smallest North American area?

   _____

4. What Native Americans were the early inhabitants of North Dakota, South Dakota, Nebraska, and Kansas?

   _____

Product Maps

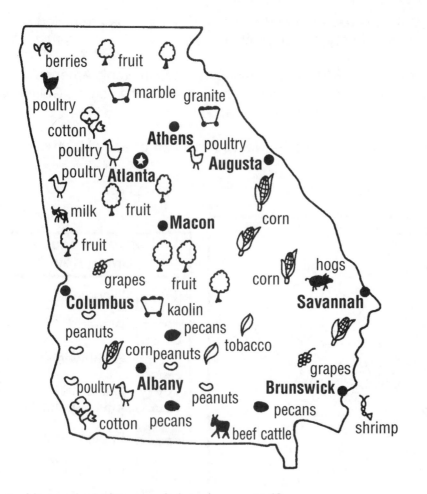

Sometimes maps can show us the types of things that are grown, raised, or mined in a certain place. These maps are called **product maps**.

Here are some of the products that are grown, raised, or mined in Georgia. Use the information on the map to answer the questions below.

1. Near what city are shrimp harvested? _____

2. What product is produced in great quantity near Macon? _____

3. What products are grown more in the southern part of Georgia than in the northern part? Name three.

   a. _____   b. _____   c. _____

4. What product is produced in the northwest corner of Georgia that is not produced in any great quantity in other locations in Georgia? _____

   _____

5. What food is grown between Augusta and Savannah? _____

6. What types of products are mined in the northern part of the state? _____

   _____

Challenge: After you have finished, use an encyclopedia or other source to find a product map of the place you live. Redraw it, selecting 10 to 20 products to draw on your map.

Population Maps

A **population map** shows the areas in which people live. This map shows the average number of people who live in certain areas of California. It is called a population density map.

Use the map to answer these questions. Write your answers on another piece of paper.

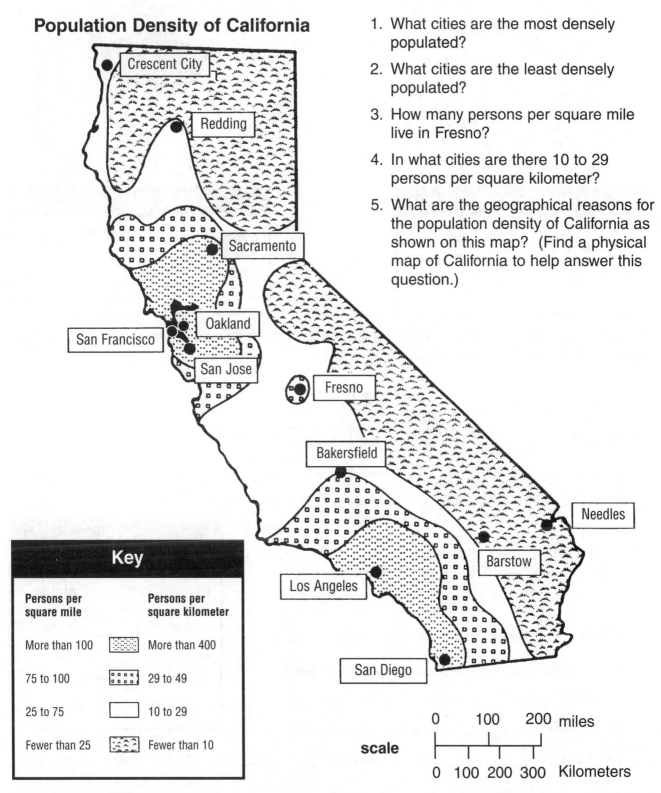

Population Density of California

1. What cities are the most densely populated?

2. What cities are the least densely populated?

3. How many persons per square mile live in Fresno?

4. In what cities are there 10 to 29 persons per square kilometer?

5. What are the geographical reasons for the population density of California as shown on this map? (Find a physical map of California to help answer this question.)

Key

Persons per square mile		Persons per square kilometer
More than 100		More than 400
75 to 100		29 to 49
25 to 75		10 to 29
Fewer than 25		Fewer than 10

scale

0   100   200 miles

0 100 200 300 Kilometers

Weather Maps

Weather maps show what the weather of a specific area has been or could be. Weather patterns are shown on maps by using symbols or shading.

February Weather in Rainier County February, 19, 1988

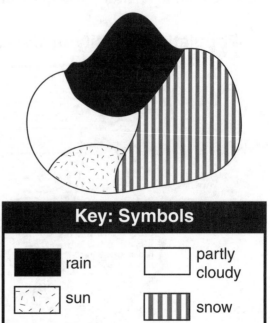

Key: Symbols

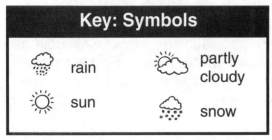

rain

partly cloudy

sun

snow

Key: Symbols

rain

partly cloudy

sun

snow

Weather maps can also show average temperatures in a specific area. Here is a map of the average January temperatures in Massachusetts.

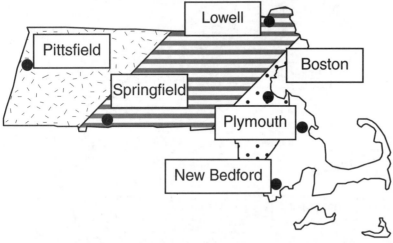

Key		
Degrees Fahrenheit		**Degrees Celsius**
Above 30		Above -1
26 to 30		-3 to -1
22 to 26		-6 to -3
Below 22		Below -6

1. Which city is coldest in January? _____

2. Which cities are in the region that has the mildest
    winters? _____

3. What is the average January temperature in

    a. Boston? _____   b. Lowell?_____   c. Pittsfield?_____

It All Adds Up!

The map skills you have learned in this book all add up! Can you read this map?

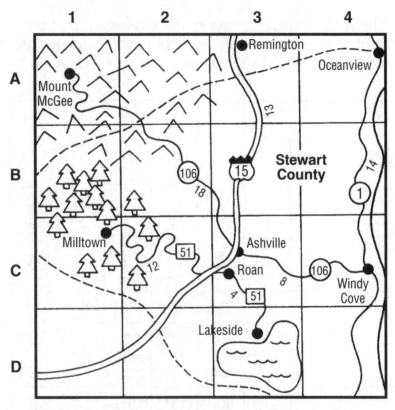

1. At what gridpoints are the following places:

   a. Lakeside _____   b. Mount McGee_____   c. Ashville and Roan_____

2. What gridpoints are completely out of Stewart County? _____

3. What type of road leads from Windy Cove to Mount McGee?_____

4. Lumber products might be milled in what grid points?_____

5. What cities are not in Stewart County? _____

6. How many miles is it from:

   a. Lakeside to Milltown? _____   b. Oceanview to Ashville? _____

7. State Highway 1 parallels what kind of land? _____

How Far to New York?

Distance charts show you the distance between two places if you travel by road.

This distance chart shows the road distances in miles between ten North American cities. Look at the chart carefully. Read it by using two fingers and coming together to find the distance between cities. Practice. When you are comfortable using the chart, answer the questions below.

Ten City Distance Chart	Albuquerque	Boston	Chicago	Denver	Indianapolis	Los Angeles	Miami	Montreal	New York City
Boston	2172		963	1949	906	2779	1504	318	206
Chicago	1281	963		996	181	2054	1329	828	802
Denver	417	1949	996		1058	1059	2037	1815	1771
Indianapolis	1266	906	181	1058		2073	1148	840	713
Los Angeles	807	2779	2054	1059	2073		2687	2873	2786
Miami	1938	1504	1329	2037	1148	2687		1654	1308
Montreal	2087	318	828	1815	840	2873	1654		378
New York City	1979	206	802	1771	713	2786	1308	378	
Seattle	1440	2976	2013	1307	2194	1311	3273	2685	2815

Find the distances between these cities:

1. Los Angeles and New York: _____

2. Seattle and Albuquerque: _____

3. Boston and New York: _____

4. Denver and Miami: _____

5. New York City and Chicago: _____

6. Montreal and Indianapolis: _____

7. Chicago and Miami: _____

8. Indianapolis and Denver: _____

9. Montreal and Los Angeles: _____

10. Seattle and Boston: _____

11. Chicago and Boston: _____

12. Denver and Albuquerque: _____

Tables

A **table** is a type of chart that is organized in such a way as to make information easy to find.

Read this table about the three major classifications of rocks. Use the information in the table to answer the questions at the bottom of this page.

Three Major Classifications of Rocks			
Classification	**rock**	**color**	**structure**
Igneous Rock (forms from hardened magma)	granite	white to gray, pink to red	closely arranged medium-to-coarse crystals
	obsidian	black, sometimes with brown streaks	glassy, no crystals
	pumice	grayish-white	light, fine pores, floats on water
Sedimentary Rock (formed by hardening of plant, animal, and mineral materials)	coal	shiny to dull black	brittle, in seams of layers
	limestone	white, gray, and buff to black and red	dense, forms cliffs, and may contain fossils
	shale	yellow, red, gray, green, black	dense, fine particles, soft, smells like clay
Metamorphic Rock (formed by existing rock changing because of heat or pressure)	marble	many colors, often mixed	medium-to-coarse crystals
	quartzite	white, gray, pink, and buff	big, hard, and often glassy
	schist	white, gray, red, green, black	flaky, banded, sparkles with mica

1. What is the name of the igneous rock that is black and has a glassy appearance?

   _____

2. What classification of rock is most likely to contain fossils?

   _____

3. To which classification do schist and marble belong?

   _____

Chart the Read-a-Thon!

Students at Hudson Elementary School have been participating in a Read-a-Thon to raise money for their school library. Each student has tallied the number of books he or she has read and is ready to collect the pledge money.

This chart represents the reading and pledging of 15 students involved in the Read-a-Thon. After reading the chart, answer the questions at the bottom of the page.

Hudson Elementary School Read-a-Thon: Room 3			
Student's Name	**Total Books Read**	**Pledge per Book**	**Money Collected**
Acevedo, Jennifer	31	10¢	$3.10
Adams, Joseph	5	10¢	$.50
Barton, Michael	61	5¢	$3.05
Duran, Louis	17	15¢	$2.55
Edwards, Marylou	47	5¢	$2.35
Harrison, Trevor	11	25¢	$2.75
Lee, Rebecca	40	10¢	$4.00
Logan, Cassie	22	5¢	$1.10
Marshall, Barbara	9	50¢	$4.50
Peterson, David	102	5¢	$5.10
Ross, Kathryn	58	10¢	$5.80
Rublo, Anthony	83	5¢	$4.15
Shea, Sharon	39	10¢	$3.90
Tran, Alvan	14	10¢	$1.40
Yetter, Liz	75	5¢	$3.75
Total	614		$48.00

1. Which student read the most books?_____

2. What was the highest amount of money collected by one student? _____

3. Who had the highest pledge of money per book? _____

4. Was the person who read the most books the same as the person who collected the most money? _____

5. Was the person who had the highest pledge of money per book the same as the person who collected the most money?_____

6. What was the total number of books read by these students? _____

7. How much money did these students earn for the library? _____

Would a Read-a-Thon be a good way to raise money at your school?

Time Line

A **time line** is a way to show events that happened in the order they happened. You read time lines from left to right.

Read this time line and then answer the questions.

School Party Time Line

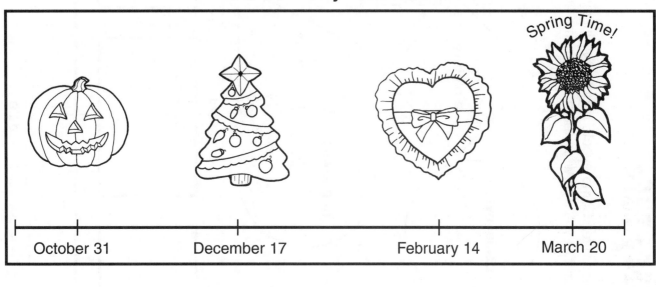

| October 31 | December 17 | February 14 | March 20 |

1. What party came first this school year?_____

2. What party came last this year?_____

3. What kind of party did the children have on February 14? _____

4. How many parties did the class have this year? _____

Make a time line using your birthday and the birthday dates of two other people in your family. Write the birthdays on the time line below. Illustrate your time line.

_____   _____   _____
         date   date   date

Events in My Life

Work with your family to find the dates for very special events in your life. Some events might have just your age or a grade level. Then choose the five events that you think are most important to you and write them on the time line below.

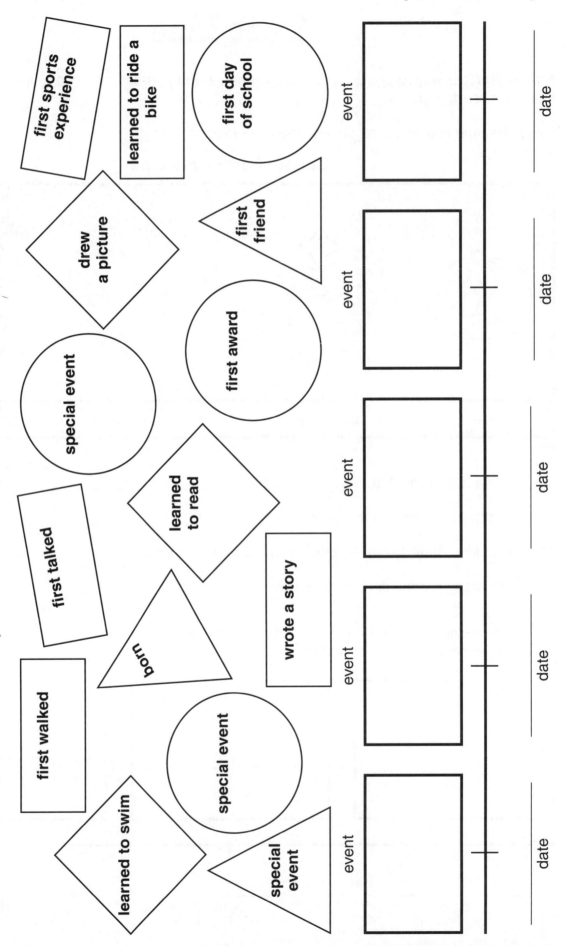

first sports experience

learned to ride a bike

first day of school

drew a picture

first friend

special event

first award

first talked

learned to read

wrote a story

born

first walked

learned to swim

special event

special event

event

event

event

event

event

date

date

date

date

date

© Teacher Created Materials, Inc.

Pictographs

One type of graph that gives us information is called a **pictograph**. In a pictograph, pictures are used instead of numbers.

Read this pictograph to find out the number and types of instruments sold in April at Harmony Music Store.

April Instrument Sales at Harmony Music Store
pianos
flutes
guitars
drums
trumpets
Key: 1 instrument = 5 instruments

1. How many of each of these instruments were sold?

   pianos _____ flutes _____ guitars _____

   drums _____ trumpets _____

2. How many more guitars were sold than . . .

   pianos? _____ flutes? _____

   drums? _____ trumpets? _____

3. Do you think the piano sales or the guitar sales brought in more money for Harmony Music Store? Explain the reason(s) for your choice.

   _____

   _____

Diagrams

Diagrams are pictures that are labeled so that a reader can easily learn the parts of what is pictured.

Do you know anything about guitars? Did you know there are different types of guitars? Can you describe the similarities and differences between acoustic and electric guitars?

Study these diagrams. Then answer the questions at the bottom of the page.

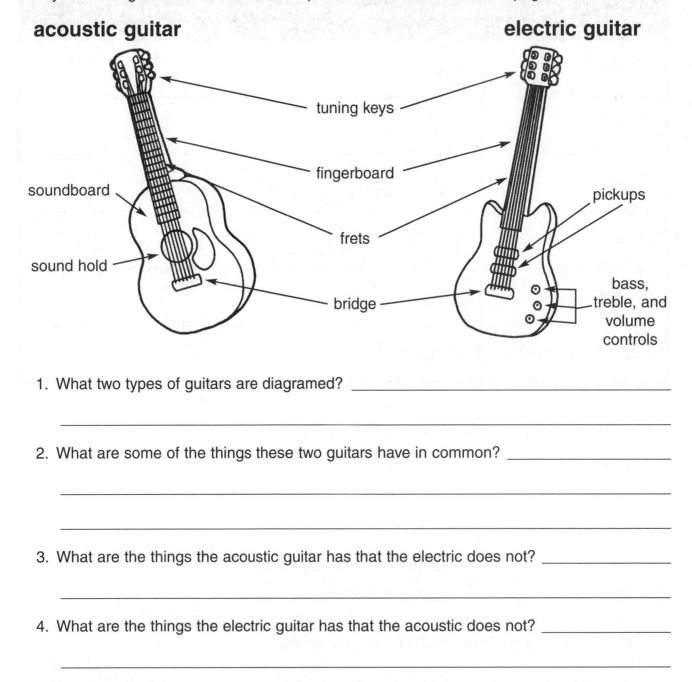

1. What two types of guitars are diagramed? _____

_____

2. What are some of the things these two guitars have in common? _____

_____

_____

3. What are the things the acoustic guitar has that the electric does not? _____

_____

4. What are the things the electric guitar has that the acoustic does not? _____

_____

*As an extension of this activity, research how a sound is made by each guitar. Then, if possible, bring acoustic and electric guitars to class for demonstration purposes.

Ant City!

Have you ever wondered what it looks like inside an ant hill? You will get an idea from studying this cutaway diagram.

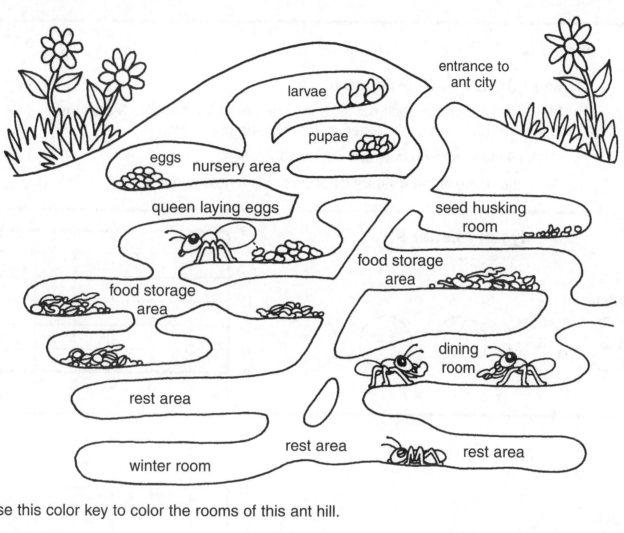

Use this color key to color the rooms of this ant hill.

| yellow | nursery area (eggs, pupae, larvae) | blue | rest area | orange | food storage area |
| purple | winter room | green | seed husking room | red | dining room |

Think about it: Why do you think the nursery is at the top of the ant city and the winter room is at the bottom?

_____

_____

_____

Graph Game

There are some letters of the alphabet hidden in these three graphs. Can you make the dots and draw the lines to find them?

Directions:

1. Begin on the left side of the graph.

2. Match the number in each pair with the number at the bottom. Match the letter in each pair with the letter on the left side of the graph.

3. Mark all the pairs with dots and connect the lines.

4. Write the name of the mystery letter on the line next to the graph.

Mystery Letter #1

Clues:

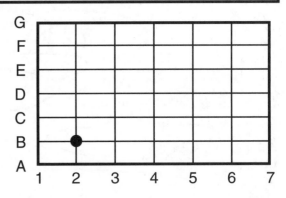

Mystery Letter #2

Clues:

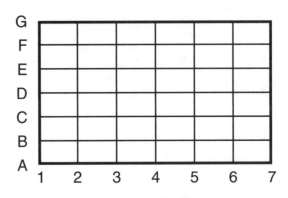

Mystery Letter #3

Clues:

  5,F

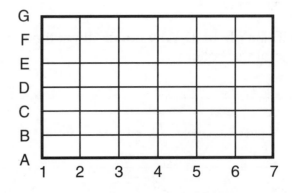

Movie Schedule

Sometimes a movie schedule is called a **timetable**. This is because the times that movies begin are listed together on a table. Look at the movie schedule. Use it to answer the questions below.

Movie	Starting Show Time
A Lad, Dan	11:00 AM, 2:00 PM, 4:30 PM
Free Billy	11:00 AM, 3:30 PM, 7:00 PM
The Sandy Lot	1:00 PM, 5:00 PM, 8:00 PM
The Mystery Garden	2:00 PM, 5:30 pm, 9:00 PM
The Adam's Farm	3:00 PM, 6:00 PM, 7:30 PM

1. Could you see *Free Billy* at 2:00 PM? _____

2. If you do not get out of church until 2:00 PM, when is the earliest you can see

   The Sandy Lot? _____

3. Is it true that three of the movies are shown in the morning? _____

   _____

4. Name the two movies that are shown at 2:00 PM. _____

   _____

5. Which movies begin after 7:30 PM? _____

   _____

6. Which movies would you like to see and at which times? _____

   _____

Go East!

Do you know where the states of the United States are in relation to each other? Now it is your chance to find out. Go east!

This is a maze game. The object of the game is to move geographically east through the states of the United States written here. Begin at Alaska and end at Maine. You may move right, left, or down. You may not move upward or diagonally. Trace your path as you go. Have a nice trip!

Start

South Carolina	Wisconsin	North Dakota	★ Alaska	Washington	Hawaii
Idaho	Virginia	New Jersey	Mississippi	Oregon	Nevada
Ohio	Colorado	Wyoming	Oklahoma	South Dakota	Montana
Maryland	Missouri	Illinois	Arkansas	Utah	California
Iowa	New Mexico	Kentucky	Georgia	Texas	North Carolina
Florida	Arizona	New York	West Virginia	Kansas	Louisiana
Maine ★	New Hampshire	Vermont	Nebraska	Indiana	Delaware

Finish

Go West!

Do you know where the countries of the world are in relation to each other? Now is your chance to find out. Go west!

This is a maze game. The object of the game is to move geographically west through the countries of the world written here. Begin at Finland and end at Canada. You may not move upward or diagonally. Trace your path as you go. Bon voyage!

Start

Russia	Spain	United States	Libya	★ Finland	Iran
Turkey	Peru	Venezuela	England	Germany	China
Nepal	Mexico	Algeria	Sudan	Japan	Brazil
Ecuador	New Zealand	Australia	Costa Rica	Thailand	Norway
Romania	Panama	Mongolia	India	Pakistan	Chile
Greece	Iraq	Sweden	Cuba	Saudi Arabia	Egypt
Canada ✪	Iceland	Ireland	France	Italy	Chad

Finish

Country and City Match

Match the city to its country by drawing a line between them.

Cities	Countries
Los Angeles	France
Glasgow	South Korea
Seoul	United States
Bombay	Japan
Nagano	Australia
Nice	Israel
Frankfurt	Portugal
Florence	Ireland
Toronto	Brazil
Lima	Peru
Rio de Janeiro	Colombia
Bogotá	Egypt
Lisbon	South Africa
Cairo	Canada
Jerusalem	Scotland
Copenhagen	Italy
Canberra	Denmark
Dublin	Mexico
Cape Town	Germany
Acapulco	India

286
© *Teacher Created Materials, Inc.*

Where Am I?

Here are clues to help you find a mystery state. When you have discovered the state, write its name on the bottom of the page.

1. I am east of California.

2. I am neither among the smallest nor the largest of the states in the United States.

3. I have a mild climate.

4. I contain all the raw materials for making steel—limestone, iron ore, and coal.

5. I am covered by forests on about two-thirds of my land.

6. I produce many chickens, eggs, and milk.

7. I am south of Michigan.

8. I have more than one famous cave.

9. I am crossed by the Tennessee River.

10. I am north of Florida.

11. I am a Southeast State.

12. I am surrounded by four states.

13. I have a belt of black clay soil that crosses me.

14. I am west of Georgia.

15. I touch the Gulf of Mexico.

I am _____!

Locate and then color the mystery state on the map below.

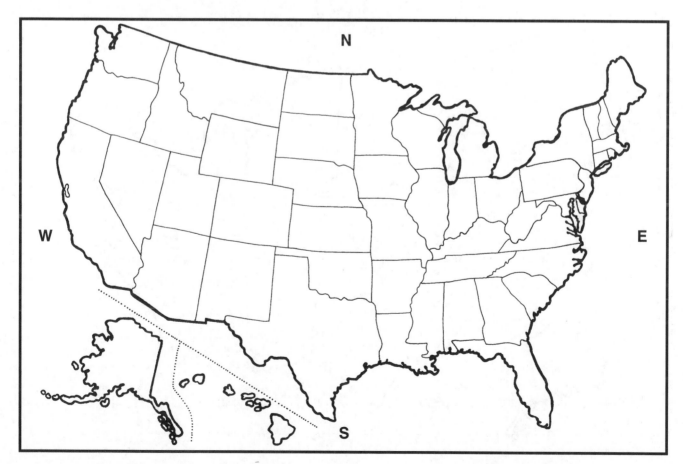

"State" My Name

Here are clues to help you find a mystery state. When you have discovered the state, write its name on the bottom of the page.

1. I am west of Virginia.

2. I am not among the smallest states in the United States.

3. I am home to buffalo, black bears, and tortoises.

4. I have a very large lake.

5. I am east of California.

6. I have rich mineral deposits, including oil shale.

7. I contain more than one national park.

8. I have snow-covered mountains.

9. I am south of Montana.

10. I am a Mountain West state.

11. I contain a huge desert.

12. I am crossed by the Colorado River.

13. I am surrounded by six states.

14. I have many famous canyons.

15. I am north of Arizona.

I am _____!

Locate and then color the mystery state on the map below.

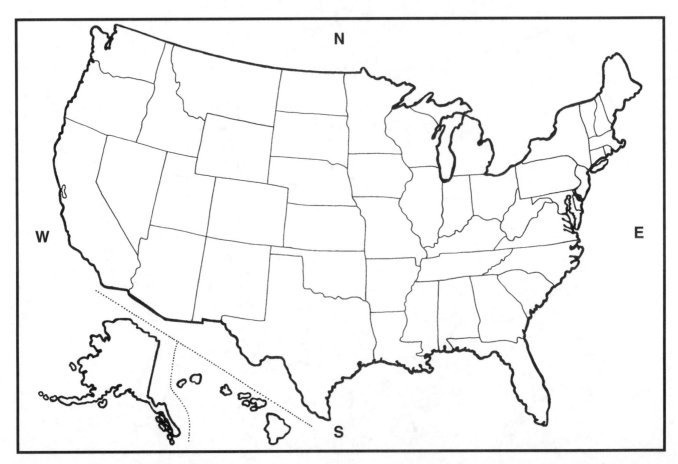

What Country Am I?

Here are clues to help you find a mystery country. When you have discovered the country, write its name on the bottom of the page.

1. I am in the Western Hemisphere.
2. I am south of Canada.
3. I am bordered by the Atlantic Ocean.
4. I am a leading producer of wheat.
5. I am north of Antarctica.
6. Early explorers came to find silver in my land.
7. I am a great world producer of cattle and sheep.
8. I am on the continent of South America.

9. I am bordered by the Andes Mountains.
10. I am in summer when the United States and Canada are in winter.
11. I am about a third the size of the United States.
12. I am bordered by the Uruguay River.
13. I have the highest and lowest elevations in South America.
14. Cape Horn is at my base.
15. I am east of Chile.

I am _____!

Use the map below to discover what the mystery country is.

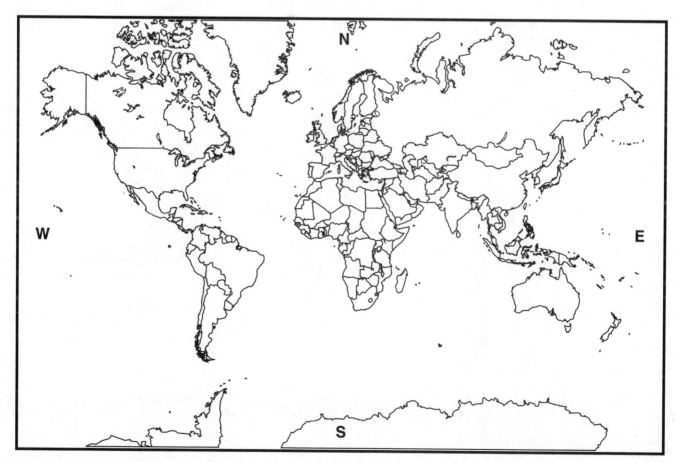

A Mystery Country

Here are clues to help you find a mystery country. When you have discovered the country, write its name on the bottom of the page.

1. I am in the Eastern Hemisphere.

2. I am not among the largest countries in the world.

3. I am west of Asia.

4. I am one of the world's leading producers and exporters of petroleum.

5. I am north of Angola.

6. Because of my nearness to the equator, I have a tropical climate.

7. I have many varied land regions.

8. I am on the continent of Africa.

9. Cacao, palm oil, and peanuts are some of my chief agricultural products.

10. I am on the west coast of Africa.

11. I rank among the world's largest nations in population.

12. Lake Chad forms part of my border.

13. I am surrounded by four countries.

14. I am crossed by the Niger River.

15. I am north of Cameroon.

I am _____!

Use the map below to discover what the mystery country is.

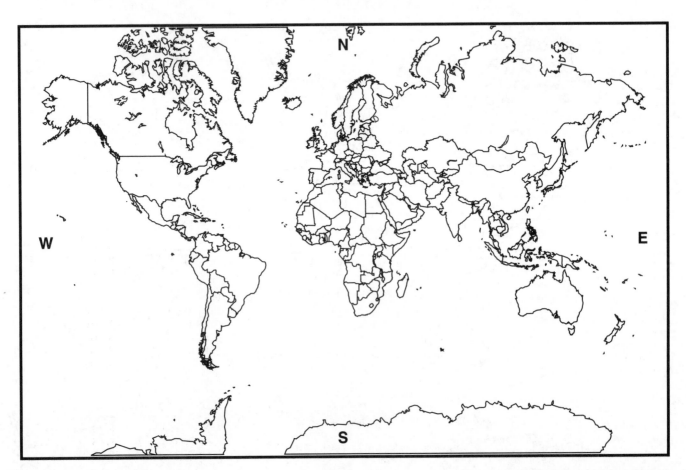

Answer Key

Page 5
1. dog, cat, tree
2. leaves, trees, wind
3. brother, baseball
4. pictures, paints
5. freedom, something, country.
6. love, family
7. electricity, light
8. student, story, rabbit, fox
9. soldiers, home, land
10. girl, money, bank
11. boys, desk, project
12. monkeys, vines, jungle
13. braid, ribbon
14. team, record, team
15. museum, exhibit

Page 6
Answers will vary.

Page 7
1. I live in the last (house) on Elm Street.
2. My (dog,) Max, and I went for a walk.
3. There are several Ryans in my (class.)
4. My (family) is planning a (trip) to the Grand Canyon.
5. "(Mom,) where is my yellow (shirt)?" Jenny asked her (mother.)
6. Where is Primrose Park?
7. The only (vegetable) I like is (broccoli.)
8. Our (cat) is named Sylvester.
9. My (teacher) is Mrs. Simms.
10. Ricky, Sam, and Tim played (football) in the (park.)
11. Katie and Emily live in Jasper City, but their (cousins) live in Walton.
12. My (brother) and his (friend) liked the (rollercoaster) at the Maple County Fair.
13. March was too windy this (year,) but April was a beautiful (month.)
14. Brent and Kenneth played (basketball) last Saturday.
15. Have the (children) ever seen *Star Wars*?

Page 8
There may be some variation in the answers; however, these are the likeliest choices.
1. clowder of cats
2. gang of elk
3. school of fish
4. tribe of monkeys
5. murder of crows
6. flight of swallows
7. pod of whales
8. crash of rhinoceroses

Page 9
1. markets
2. pencils
3. trucks
4. farmers
5. cupcakes
6. students
7. telephones
8. computers
9. pictures
10. penguins

Page 10
1. parties
2. companies
3. armies
4. countries
5. spies
6. puppies
7. liberties
8. flies
9. berries
10. factories
11. flurries
12. families
13. stories
14. victories
15. babies
16. ladies
17. monoplies
18. bodies

Page 11
1. dishes (*color*)
2. circuses (*color*)
3. parties
4. babies
5. buzzes (*color*)
6. inches (*color*)
7. keys
8. passes (*color*)
9. classes (*color*)
10. clowns
11. coaches (*color*)
12. watches (*color*)
13. fishes (*color*)
14. pitches (*color*)
15. finches (*color*)

Page 12
bush, bushes; pen, pens; bench, benches; egg, eggs; match, matches; miss, misses; valley, valleys; worry, worries; flower, flowers; princess, princesses; address, addresses; peach, peaches

Page 13
Sentences will vary.
1. men
2. women
3. children
4. sheep
5. mice
6. feet
7. oxen
8. geese

Page 14
1. doll's
2. Lena's
3. girls'
4. turtle's
5. Kate's
6. child's
7. boys'
8. penguin's
9. blouse's
10. pan's
11. man's
12. Jen's
13. lions'
14. toys'
15. play's

Page 15
1. plays
2. flies
3. makes
4. ran
5. popped
6. ran
7. fell
8. eat
9. stood
10. reads

Page 16
woke, jumped, landed, sat, rubbed, grumbled, fell, looked, wanted, see, ran, grabbed, blew, played, liked, sounded, heard, stopped, listened, came, like, grabbed, ran, sat, played, floated, felt, heard, stopped, listened, came, ran, played, liked, heard, called, went, took, put, put, told, went, tried, imagine, heard, stopped, listened, snored, moaned, stuck, heard, covered, fell

Page 17

Helping Verbs	Action Verbs
1. will	1. ride
2. is	2. ridden
3. were	3. pushed
4. can	4. move
5. has	5. driven
6. have	6. pulled
7. have	7. seen
8. will	8. go
9. is	9. going
10. will	10. drink

Page 18
1. painted
2. climbed
3. played
4. laughed
5. shouted
6. jumped
7. ran
8. saw
9. ate
10. came
11. made
12. built
13. slept
14. gave
15. took
16. brought
17. sang
18. held
19. went
20. wrote

Page 19
1. turned
2. cooked
3. rolled
4. watched
5. parked
6. filled
7. colored
8. folded
9. closed
10. looked
11. smile
12. fold
13. close
14. paint
15. climb
16. share
17. joke
18. match
19. laugh
20. play

Page 20
1. blew
2. came
3. sang
4. wore
5. took
6. cried
7. made
8. gave
9. fell
10. flew
11. catch
12. read
13. ride
14. drink
15. swing
16. shine
17. pay
18. write
19. sweep
20. tear

Page 21
1. was
2. were
3. was
4. were
5. was
6. were
7. were
8. was
9. were
10. was

Page 22
1. are
2. are
3. am
4. is
5. are
6. are
7. are
8. is
9. am
10. am

Page 23
1. S, has
2. P, run
3. P, jump
4. S, hops
5. P, sing
6. S, is
7. P, are
8. S, hops
9. S, is
10. S, has

© *Teacher Created Materials, Inc.*   291   *Practice and Learn—Fourth Grade*

Answer Key (cont.)

Page 24
1. unusual, front
2. playful
3. green, long
4. funny, old
5. new, gray
6. tall, pretty.
7. smart, funny
8. silly
9. happy, large
10. small, black, shiny
11. choir, colorful, lively
12. kind, generous
13. orange, yellow
14. little, imaginary
15. quiet, barn

Page 25
1. this; Which one?
2. old; What kind of?
3. French; What kind of?
4. Scottish; What kind of?
5. yellow; What kind of?
6. three; How many?
7. delicious, spinach; What kind of?
8. comic; What kind of?
9. soft; What kind of?
10. mean; What kind of?
11. clueless; What kind of?
12. those, black, small; What kind of?

Page 26
Adjectives will vary.

Page 27
1. a
2. an
3. a
4. an
5. a
6. a
7. an
8. an
9. a
10. a
11. An
12. a
13. a
14. An
15. A

Page 28
1. taller, tallest
2. sweeter, sweetest
3. smaller, smallest
4. messier, messiest
5. bigger, biggest
6. prettier, prettiest
7. harder, hardest
8. thicker, thickest

Page 29
1. how; quietly
2. when; tomorrow
3. when; later
4. where; here
5. how; fiercely
6. how; softly
7. how; gracefully
8. when; Yesterday
9. how; well
10. how; quickly

Page 30
Verbs and adverbs will vary.

Page 31
Answers may vary but here are some possibilities.
1. trustingly
2. calmly
3. sharply
4. permanently
5. truthfully
6. patiently
7. correctly
8. carefully
9. quietly
10. lightly

Page 32
1. He played baseball.
2. She swam across the pool.
3. They climbed the trees.
4. They rode their bikes to school.
5. The team surprised her with a trophy.
6. Kim saw it run across the street.
7. She read the new best seller.
8. He saw a strange shadow.
9. The girls walked to her house.
10. The family found them in a basket on their porch.
11. Where should I put them?
12. He put gas in the car.
13. They won the championship!
14. Where is it?
15. Please, give that to him.

Page 33
Answers will vary.

Page 34
1. busy, active
2. nibble, chew
3. flavorful, tasty
4. joyful, happy
5. fall, trip
6. huge, enormous
7. worried, anxious
8. mad, angry
9. talk, chat
10. cry, weep

Page 35
1. neat, spotless
2. sad, unhappy
3. thin, skinny
4. look, see
5. plain, simple
6. strong, powerful
7. cold, chilly
8. big, large
9. cheap, stingy
10. quiet, calm
11. poor, needy
12. little, small
13. sharp, pointed
14. loud, noisy
15. rich, wealthy

Page 36
1. like, similar
2. snip, cut
3. plump, fat
4. fly, soar
5. bark, yelp
6. clown, jester
7. huge, gigantic
8. real, true
9. entire, whole
10. baby, infant

Page 37
1. laugh, cry
2. fast, slow
3. hurt, heal
4. shiny, dull
5. wake, sleep
6. girl, boy
7. fire, water
8. truth, lie
9. ugly, pretty
10. hard, soft

Page 38
Answers will vary but may include:
1. hard
2. sour
3. cold
4. later
5. lie
6. mean
7. murky
8. west

Page 40
1. hare, hair
2. our, hour
3. dough, doe
4. no, know
5. read, red
6. tale, tail

Page 41
1. might
2. not
3. popular
4. plum
5. bare
6. bawl
7. banned
8. franc
9. cymbal
10. chilly
11. scent
12. hymn
13. bazaar
14. blue
15. cereal

Page 42
1. Weather Flash . . . heavy rains due in an hour.
2. Next, on *The World Turns* . . . Elizabeth is never seen again.
3. News Extra! A wild horse and deer escape from zoo.
4. Watch Muscle Man weekly lift weights on Channel 2.
5. Special Announcement! Ice skating pair wins gold medals!
6. Try a new cereal just for kids! *Awesome Oats!*

Page 43
1. S
2. S
3. A
4. S
5. A
6. A
7. A
8. S
9. S
10. S
11. A
12. A
13. S
14. S
15. A
16. A
17. S
18. A
19. A
20. S

Page 44
1. antonym
2. synonym
3. antonym
4. homophone
5. synonym
6. homophone
7. homophone
8. synonym
9. antonym
10. synonym
11. homophone
12. antonym
13. antonym
14. synonym
15. homophone
16. antonym
17. antonym
18. homophone
19. synonym
20. antonym

Answer Key (cont.)

Page 45
Some answers will vary.
Sunday, Monday, Tuesday, Wednesday,
Thursday, Friday, Saturday
1. January
2. February
3. March
4. April
5. May
6. June
7. July
8. August
9. September
10. October
11. November
12. December

Page 46
Pacific Ocean, Grand Canyon, Mt. Rushmore, Amazon River, Sahara Desert, North Pole, San Diego Zoo, Lake Louise, Rocky Mountains, Hyde Park, Disneyland, Niagara Falls

Page 47
One, When, What, Mike, It's, Both, Ohhh, It's, Sure, Mike, Chris, Mike, He, The, Nobody, Mike, Chris, Next, The, No, You, Why, We, Well, The, They, They, George

Page 48
1. Uncle Jorge sat on the front porch.
2. I said, "Mom, what I really want to do is to stay home!"
3. My mom and my dad won't be home until 7 P.M.
4. His grandma made a quilt for his birthday.
5. My cousin and my grandma will be coming with my mom.
6. Our grandparents have a surprise for Aunt Aimee.
7. I wrote "Dear Grandma," at the top of my stationery.
8. I wish my aunt lived closer to us; she looks just like Mom.
9. Then Dad stopped and looked behind him.
10. I like to go to Grandmother Norton's house in the summer.
11. My favorite cousin is Jimmy because he makes me laugh.
12. At the wedding we saw Aunt Marsha and Cousin Brad.
13. My mom and dad are taking me to dinner after the awards assembly.
14. At the reunion I saw Aunt Edith, Uncle Jacques, and Cousins Kathy, Meredith, Hector, and Samantha.
15. For my birthday I'm inviting Cousin Sarah, Cousin Leigh, Aunt Susie, and my uncle, whose name is Mike.

Page 49
1. isn't
2. let's
3. can't
4. he'll
5. aren't
6. we've

Page 50
1. couldn't
2. haven't
3. can't
4. aren't
5. isn't
6. wouldn't

Page 51
1. do not
2. would not
3. will not
4. are not
5. should not
6. he is
7. I have
8. they have
9. we are
10. she is
11. you will
12. did not
13. is not
14. was not
15. we will
16. I would

Page 52
cannot, You are, Do not, will not, could not, it is, it is, that is, Let us, it is, will not, must have, I had, must have, she would, did not, There have, who have, must have, should not, could not, It is, would have, that is, I had, she had, she would, I will, would have, was not, were not, Who is, we are, would have, was not, could not, should not, would not, What is, must not, were not, would have, she had, had not, she had, she would, Here is, it is, She has, She has, I am, I will

Page 53
1. !
2. . or !
3. ?
4. .
5. .
6. ?
7. ?
8. !
9. .
10. . or !
11. !
12. ! or .
13. ?
14. .
15. ?

Page 54
1. . . . Amy, Katy, and Melissa.
2. . . . basketball, baseball, and volleyball.
3. Katy, Melissa, and Tommy . . .
4. . . . a geologist, an astronaut, or a chemist.
5. . . . Skip, Tiger, and Rags.
6. . . . math, science, and art.
7. Tommy, Amy, Katy, and Melissa . . .
8. . . . his parents, his sisters, and his dogs.
9. . . . three birds, two cats, and one dog.
10. . . . Tommy, Amy, and Manuel.

Page 55
1. Mrs. Burnett, may we go out to recess now?
2. Yes, we are going out to recess now, Jason.
3. Mary, will you swing with Tommy and me?
4. Sure, Jason, I love to swing.
5. Mary is going to swing with us, Tommy.
6. No, Jason, I'm sliding with Matt.
7. Matt can swing with us, Tommy.
8. Jason, we can all swing first, and then we can all slide.
9. Jason, do you want to go on the slide first?
10. Tommy, what time is recess over?

Page 56
1. Amy Jones, my best friend, has a very large family.
2. Joe, her oldest brother, works for an airline company.
3. The youngest in the family, Tony, is only three years old.
4. The oldest daughters, Karen and Sue, often help with the younger children.
5. My other good friend, Nicole, and I spend a great deal of time at Amy's house.
6. Mrs. Jones, Amy's mother, says that two more children are coming tomorrow.
7. Amy's dad, Mr. Jones, works hard to take care of seven children.
8. Rags and Slick, the Jones' pets, get a great deal of attention.

Page 57
1. Jerry was born on October 5, 1986.
2. My favorite Christmas was December 25, 1992.
3. Susan's mom came home from the hospital on April 6, 1994.
4. We took our summer vacation on July 21, 1993.
5. My grandfather was born on August 11, 1941.
6. On April 6, 1994, Susan's mom brought a new baby girl home from the hospital.
7. My grandfather remembers July 20, 1969, as an important date in history.
8. On July 21, 1993, my family went to Hawaii for our summer vacation.

Page 58
1. The state capital is in Austin, Texas.
2. My home is in Denver, Colorado.
3. Her grandparents live in Bangor, Maine.
4. Our tournament is in Ardmore, Oklahoma.
5. Disney World is in Orlando, Florida.
6. Her father is stationed in Fairbanks, Alaska.
7. Queen Elizabeth lives in London, England.
8. We rode the ferry in Seattle, Washington.

Page 59
1. April 15, 1972
2. July 27, 1640
3. September 13, 1910
4. Monday, January 31
5. Sunday, November 16
6. Anaheim, California
7. Albuquerque, New Mexico
8. Quebec, Canada
9. Bangor, Maine
10. Little Rock, Arkansas
11. Dear Joe,
12. Your friend,
13. Sincerely yours,
14. Love,
15. Yours truly,
16. All birds have feathers, wings, and beaks.
17. The Shetland pony is small, friendly, and gentle.
18. A friendly, playful dog makes a good pet.
19. I have three cats named Boots, Muffin, and Tiger.
20. I like to color with pencils, markers, and crayons.

Answer Key (cont.)

Page 60
1. No, Marlene does not like being squirted in the face.
2. Christopher, how long have you been on the telephone?
3. Well, just what did you have in mind?
4. Sure, Laura, I'd love another jelly donut.
5. My brother, the world's scariest boy, likes escargots.
6. The plane we are taking, a 747, will have plenty of room.
7. You realize, of course, that you will not be allowed out of the house in that outfit.
8. My orthodontist, Dr. Baugh, decorated his office for Halloween.
9. All right, if that's what you think, let's just eat all of the chocolate.
10. In the future we will be able to speak to our computers.
11. No kidding, you went rock climbing?
12. We went to Bouquet Canyon, a canyon near Valencia, to attend a harvest festival.
13. You could read, for example, some books about the historical period in which your novel takes place.
14. For Valentine's Day my dad gave me two pounds of my favorite treat, candy corn.
15. I don't care what you think, I'm going to go back there and help that little boy.

Page 61
1. cat's food
2. bird's nest
3. Miguel's bike
4. Kim's store
5. David's CD player
6. sister's book
7. brother's skateboard
8. baby's toys
9. teacher's desk
10. painter's brush
11. Nicky ran screaming into Manuel's house.
12. My dad knocked down a hornet's nest.
13. I wish I could drive my brother's car.
14. An alien ate Mariela's homework.
15. Grandpa's spaghetti is the best in the world.

Page 62
1. Ryan asked, "What do you want to play, Martha?"
2. Martha answered, "Let's play baseball."
3. "Okay, we'll play baseball first," said Ryan, "but let's play basketball after that."
4. Mom called, "The cookies are ready."
5. "Oh, boy," the boys yelled at the same time, "let's eat!"

Page 63
1. "What is that bizarre thing upon your head? It looks like an octopus," said Mr. Grimmy. (exact words)
2. The teacher told the students to read the poem, "The Raven" by Friday. (title)
3. I call my sister "Idget," but I have no idea why. (special word)

4. "Hey!" Jacques shouted, "Didn't you hear the coach? He said, 'Stop when you get to the fence!'" (quote within a quote)
5. "And then I will cover you with fragrant rose petals," Mama said, "and sing a lullaby." (exact words)
6. I found a book that said, "Dinosaurs may be more closely related to birds than to lizards." (exact words)
7. We have family nicknames, and my brother's is "Greasy Bear." (special word)
8. "Did you hear what Nicole said?" Amy asked us. "She said, 'You guys are just too chicken to try it.' She doesn't know what she is talking about!" (quote within a quote)
9. I thought you would be too "cool" to go on the merry-go-round with me. (special word)
10. She watched *Somewhere in Time* so many times she wore out the tape. (no quotation marks)
11. My brother always talks in his sleep. Last night he said, "Hurry and purple it before the snails get it!" (exact words)
12. After we watched *Twister,* we couldn't stop watching the clouds. (no quotation marks)
13. "Come with us," Dad said, "and we can stop for ice cream on the way." (exact words)
14. I need to find the root word for "transient." (special word)
15. Mom says we shouldn't say "Where's he at?" because it is not proper English. (special words)

Page 64
Dear Pen Pal,

I love to go to the circus! On May 6, 1999, the circus came to my hometown of Jackson, Wyoming. A parade marched through our streets, and soon the big top could be seen. Ken, my brother, and I went to watch the performers prepare for opening night. We saw clowns, acrobats, and even the ringmaster. What a sight! Have you ever seen anything like it? You should go if you ever get the chance.

I also really enjoy playing baseball. My favorite team is the New York Yankees, but I also like the Cardinals. When I grow up I want to be a baseball pitcher, first baseman, or shortstop. Do you like baseball? What do you want to do when you grow up? I wish you could see my cool baseball card collection, but Ken's collection is even better.

Oh, I almost forgot to tell you about my family! There are four people in my family. They are my mom, my dad, my brother, and me. Scruffy, my cat, is also a family member. In August 2000 my grandpa will probably move in with us. I can't wait for that! Didn't you say your grandma lives with you? I'll bet you really like that.

Well, that's all for now. Please write back to me soon. See you!

Your pal,
Brent

Page 65
1. Blake
2. the paintbox
3. the colors
4. Blake
5. Green
6. Orange
7. Blake
8. Blake's favorite color
9. Mom
10. The painting

Page 66
1. Kids
2. Baseball
3. Swimming
4. I
5. Summertime
6. Jeremy
7. Mosquitoes
8. my skin, I
9. seashells
10. summer, it

Page 67
1. is very cold
2. jump into the water
3. splashes us
4. is cold
5. gets out of the water
6. does a handstand underwater
7. claps for him
8. has a leak in it
9. throws the inner tube onto the shore
10. sits on the inner tube
11. deflates with Tonia on it
12. laughs with Tonia
13. jumps into the water
14. swims as fast as he can
15. races Luke

Page 68
1. (Uncle Tony) invited us to the baseball game.
2. (His truck) carried us to the field.
3. (The parking lot) was crowded.
4. (We) finally found our seats.
5. (Uncle Tommy) bought popcorn and peanuts.
6. (Two batters) hit home runs.
7. (Our team) won the game.
8. (People) pushed to get out of the stadium.
9. (We) drove home late at night.
10. (My sister) was very tired.

Page 69–72
Answers will vary.

Page 73
1. Tuesday is the day we go to the library.
2. Who is your teacher?
3. The students in my class were reading.
4. What a wonderful day it is!
5. Jordan, come play with us.
6. Watch out, Michelle!
7. Do you like math?
8. I will paint today.
9. What time is lunch?
10. I got a sticker!

Page 74
1. Gorillas eat ripe bananas.
2. The magician opened the secret door.

3. This sentence makes sense.
4. The egg broke on my head.
5. The tired dog took a nap.
6. The snake bit the zookeeper.
7. The boy sharpened his pencil.
8. The girl made a program for her computer.
9. I called my mother on the phone.
10. Susie watched the television.

Page 75

1. My books are on the table. My math book is on top.
2. They were closing the store. It was time to go home.
3. Watch out for the slippery ice! You could fall and hurt yourself.
4. I got a new blue dress. The blue shoes match perfectly.
5. My brother made the team! Will I be able to play baseball some day?
6. I like to go camping. The last time we went, we saw a bear.
7. My teacher was not at school. We had a substitute.
8. I don't like lima beans. I only want mashed potatoes.
9. Can you spend the night at my house? We can have pizza for dinner.
10. My dog has fleas. We had to get her some special medicine.

Page 76
Answers will vary.

Page 77

1. Bruce has many things in his room.
2. Answers will vary.
3. Is there a box of toys under the bed?
4. A rug is in front of the closet.
5. Answers will vary.
6. I can see trees from my window.
7. Answers will vary.
8. Answers will vary.
9. Answers will vary.
10. Latoya cleans her room every day.

Page 78

1. D		6. D	
2. I		7. I	
3. I		8. D	
4. D		9. I	
5. I		10. D	

Page 79

1–5: Answers will vary
1. I am very tired.
2. Let's sit down here.
3. What a wonderful idea!
4. Ouch!
5. Watch where you throw that ball!
6. Well, then, let's have some lunch.
7. The sandwich is for you.
8. That lasagna is very hot! (or) That lasagna is very hot.
9. I didn't think you wanted lasagna.
10. Sue would like a hamburger, please.

11. Bob, you don't have to get so upset! (or) Bob, you don't have to get so upset.
12. This sandwich tastes good.
13. I love roast beef! (or) I love roast beef.
14. Take your brother to the park.

Page 80
I went to the store because I needed to get something for lunch. My stomach was growling so much that a little boy sitting in a shopping cart could hear it. "Mom," he said, "he has a rumbly tumbly!" "Shush," said his mother. I turned to the little boy and asked, "I have a what?" "A rumbly tumbly," he said and smiled shyly. "A rumbly tumbly, a rumbly tumbly," I said over and over again. The little boy started to giggle, and I was even hungrier than before. "Yikes!" I said to the little boy. "I have to get something to eat before my rumbly tumbly tumbles!" The little boy stopped giggling, pointed his finger at me, and said, "Go get something to eat right now before your rumbly tumbly tumbles!" "Okay!" I said as I rushed down the aisle toward the apples and bananas.

Page 81

1. C, baby
2. V, egg
3. V, apple
4. C, car
5. C, lollipop (or sucker)
6. V, ostrich
7. C, tree
8. C, girl

Page 82
Answers may include the following:
bl: block, blind, blue, blow
br: brown, brook, bright, bring
cl: clown, clap, clean, clutter
cr: cry, creep, cringe, crave
dr: drive, drink, drown, drip
fl: fly, flip, flounce, flit
fr: French, fry, free, frost
gl: glee, glean, glad, glow
gr: green, grass, grow, grape
pl: please, play, plot, plan
pr: pray, prim, promise, proper
sl: slow, slide, sled, slant
sp: space, spice, sport, speck
st: stand, stop, stick, stall
str: street, strand, strap, string
tr: train, trap, trim, trout

Page 83

1. chick or thick
2. choose
3. chop, shop, or whop
4. shape
5. math or mash
6. thank or shank
7. cheese
8. check
9. thirst
10. whistle or thistle
11. bath or bash
12. wish or with

13. whip, chip, or ship
14. bench
15. washing
16. trash

Page 84
yellow = mine, nice, find, try, sigh
purple = treat, eat, free, seem, he, she, sleep, meet, bee, team
red = tape, table, name, whale, ate
green = show, open, so
blue = you, fuse, huge, cube, rule

Page 85
green = club, nut, cup
purple = cat, and, fan
blue = men, when, met
yellow = stop, pot, nod, mob, off, on
red = thin, flip, bit

Page 86
short: bat, beg, bun, fish, hot, jack, let, moth, pump, tin
long: beach, boat, cake, eat, light, maid, mule, muse, note, write

Page 87

1. cane		9. bite	
2. site		10. cube	
3. cape		11. grime	
4. tube		12. fine	
5. dote		13. bathe	
6. note		14. vane	
7. rate		15. plane	
8. lobe			

Page 88

1. write		14. batch	
2. witch		15. whip	
3. whole		16. hour	
4. dumb		17. catch	
5. knot		18. wrong	
6. notch		19. wrinkle	
7. knew		20. match	
8. comb		21. knight	
9. honest		22. knee	
10. lamb		23. crumb	
11. ghost		24. knife	
12. whale		25. thumb	
13. wrench		26. knit	

Page 89

1. alphabet		10. fun	
2. awful		11. giraffe	
3. cough		12. laugh	
4. dolphin		13. muff	
5. elephant		14. phonics	
6. elf		15. rough	
7. enough		16. taffy	
8. fantastic		17. telephone	
9. fish		18. tough	

Page 90
f sound: cough, enough, rough, slough*, tough, trough
silent: daughter, dough, knight, light, naughty, night, right, sigh, sight, slough*, taught, though
*Note that slough can be pronounced both ways, and each way has a different meaning.

Answer Key (cont.)

Page 91

1. ache
2. back
3. bank
4. beak
5. cane
6. cut
7. crumb
8. dock
9. jack
10. keep
11. key
12. kind
13. look
14. make
15. neck
16. nickel
17. pack
18. pocket
19. scare
20. school
21. skin
22. sock
23. spoke
24. stomach
25. walk
26. rake

Page 92

1. pig
2. bee or flea
3. snake
4. llama
5. bird
6. rabbit
7. horse
8. deer
9. fox or ox
10. dog, frog, or hog

1–4: Answers will vary but may include:
cat, rat, bat, gnat
goose, moose
whale, snail
hare, bear

Page 93

1. alone, known
2. bowl, roll
3. coat, wrote
4. home, roam
5. leak, week
6. maid, frayed
7. plate, great
8. seize, bees
9. sigh, fly
10. soap, rope
11. tail, bale
12. thought, taught

Page 94

1. paper
2. out
3. man
4. ball
5. moon
6. fall
7. light
8. out
9. table
10. book
11. over
12. day
13. room
14. up
15. cup

Page 95

goldfish, spotlight, sweatshirt, highway, cupcake, shoelace, railway, sunset, peppermint, football, ponytail, overlook, suitcase, jellyfish, windmill, silverware, tiptoe, rainbow, wristwatch, handlebar

Page 96

sunshine, flashlight, suitcase, tablecloth, football, raincoat, mailbox, butterfly, toothbrush, starfish, tabletop, sidewalk, mailman

Page 97

1. pil´-low
2. fel´-low
3. piz´-za
4. sup-pose´
5. sur-round´
6. scis´-sors
7. col-lect´
8. hur-rah´
9. ad´-dress or ad-dress´
10. sil´-ly

Page 98

1. tur´-tle
2. bee´-tle
3. bub´-ble
4. can´-dle
5. jug´-gle
6. hus´-tle
7. baf´-fle
8. cra´-dle
9. bot´-tle
10. trou´-ble

Page 99

1. car-toon´
2. cin´-der
3. drop´-let
4. ex´-tra
5. ex-press´
6. im-print´ or im´-print
7. jun´-gle
8. sal´-ad
9. mag´-ic
10. pic´-ture

Page 100

1. hu´-mor
2. a´-ble
3. be-gin´
4. ki´-wi
5. pa´-per
6. lo´-cate
7. o´-pen
8. pro´-file
9. ro-sette´
10. e-rupt´

Page 101

1. responsible
2. understand
3. meaning
4. worth
5. material
6. engage
7. aware
8. arrange
9. circle
10. week
11. mountain
12. cycle
13. angle
14. sense
15. admiral

Page 102

1. sail
2. run
3. farm
4. buy
5. pharmacy
6. direct
7. dance
8. science
9. photograph
10. analyze
11. choreograph
12. biography

Page 103

(un)- known, (re) - phrase, (dis) - respect, (re) - make, (pre) - cook, (mis) - align

Page 104

Answers will vary.

Page 105

1. reheat (*yellow*)
2. replay (*yellow*)
3. unsafe (*green*)
4. unlucky (*green*)
5. redo (*yellow*)
6. unfair (*green*)
7. reread (*yellow*)
8. rewrite (*yellow*)
9. uncover (*green*)

Page 106

overslept: slept too much
overstuffed: stuffed too much
underwatered: not watered enough
underfed: not fed enough
overflowed: flowed too much
undercooked: not cooked enough

Page 107

1. kind-(ness)
2. care-(ful)
3. help-(ful)
4. seed-(less)
5. clean-(ly)
6. health-(ful)

Page 108

Answers will vary.

Page 109

1. bucket; bucketful
2. spoon; spoonful
3. help; helpful
4. hand; handful
5. harm; harmful
6. pain; painful

Page 110

1. scenic
2. angelic
3. terrific
4. patriotic
5. majestic
6. traffic
7. Nomadic
8. antiseptic
9. scientific
10. volcanic

Page 111

Answers may vary but may include:

1. goose
2. summer
3. football
4. intelligence
5. doodle
6. buccaneer
7. bee
8. giraffe
9. beggar
10. moon
11. pepper
12. gaggle
13. wiggle
14. borrow
15. sorrow
16. sonnet
17. ballot
18. classic

Page 113

1. high
2. kayak
3. nitrogen
4. hopscotch
5. amnesia
6. maximum
7. dividend
8. neon
9. episode
10. hearth
11. aqua
12. newborn
13. moonbeam
14. arena
15. critic
16. Antarctica
17. Australia
18. Africa
19. Asia
20. Europe

Page 114

Answers will vary but may include:

1. canoe
2. pans
3. brain
4. low
5. lemon
6. spot
7. leaf
8. grin
9. rat
10. mug
11. earth
12. tab
13. wasp
14. pea
15. note
16. pat
17. pots
18. ton
19. rope
20. ewe

Answer Key (cont.)

Page 115
Answers will vary.

Page 116
Answers will vary. Use a dictionary to check the spelling.

Page 117
Answers will vary. Use a dictionary to check the spelling.

Page 118
1. veteran or veterinarian
2. necktie
3. moving picture
4. champion
5. photograph
6. helicopter
7. referee
8. market
9. dormitory
10. examination
11. advertisement
12. doctor
13. laboratory
14. promenade
15. influenza
16. teenager
17. gasoline
18. statistic
19. luncheon
20. chrysanthemum

Page 119
One day the fourth-grade class went on a trip to the zoo. They took a bus to get there. Then everyone joined in groups to tour the zoo. The blue group went to see the bears, the red group went to the seals, and the yellow group walked to the monkey area. At noon, all the groups met for lunch. The children ate sandwiches and drank a lot of water. After lunch, they saw a bird show in the zoo theater. When the show was over, it was time to go home. The children piled into the bus and away they went. They had a great day!

Page 120
1. n
2. b
3. h
4. e
5. l
6. j
7. f
8. a
9. o
10. d
11. m
12. i
13. k
14. g
15. c

a. Blvd.
b. Mr.
c. yr.
d. Gov.
e. Dec.
f. tbs.
g. Tues.
h. St.
i. gal.
j. Capt.
k. Dr.
l. U.S.
m. Jr.
n. Wed.
o. Aug.

Page 121
1. president
2. as soon as possible
3. adjective
4. pounds
5. maximum
6. et cetera (and so forth)
7. September
8. Master of Arts
9. I owe you.
10. Bachelor of Arts
11. cash on delivery
12. répondez síl vous plaít. (Please reply.)
13. self-addressed, stamped envelope
14. South America
15. building
16. railroad
17. preposition
18. headquarters
19. district attorney
20. daylight-savings time

Page 122
1. record´
2. de´sert
3. content´
4. con´test
5. refuse´
6. read (red)
7. close (cloz)
8. con´duct
9. sub´ject
10. address´

Page 123
1. mat
2. mate
3. tine
4. tin
5. fed
6. feed
7. us
8. use
9. meet
10. met

Page 124
1. tail or tale
2. most
3. trace
4. hazy
5. doe or dough
6. duel
7. fray
8. trail
9. replay
10. wheel
11. meter
12. motor
13. geese
14. china
15. love

Page 125
ape	kick	satisfy
apple	kiss	season
banana	laugh	state
bear	limb	town
carrot	list	tuna
cheese	many	tune
cornhusk	mote	umbrella
dandelion	mother	under
dandy	neck	underneath
egg	noise	very
eggplant	other	violin
friend	otter	voice
frond	over	wig
grapes	pout	wisdom
grass	put	wonder
heaven	putt	xylophone
house	quilt	yeast
hover	quit	yes
ice	quitter	yesterday
icicle	raise	zebra
juice	roast	zoo
jump	salt	zoology

Page 126
candy	grassy	rover
cane	house	salt
cart	join	same
cell	jump	science
cello	launch	scientist
dear	light	silent
deer	line	simple
dog	lion	sort
friend	loop	tune
gamble	lope	tunnel
game	lunch	umbrella
ghastly	moan	vest
ghost	moon	
grass	river	

Page 127
1. c
2. c
3. a
4. b
5. b

Page 128
Definitions and sentences will vary.

Page 129
A. Answers will vary.
B. 1. Wash five small, empty food containers such as yogurt cartons or margarine tubs.
   2. In each container, mix 1 teaspoon of cold cream and 2 teaspoons of cornstarch.
   3. Add 1 teaspoon of water and a few drops of food coloring to each container. Blend carefully.
   4. Be sure to use a different color for each container: blue, green, red, yellow, and brown.
   5. After creating a batch of face paint, work with a partner and paint your faces to look like zoo creatures.
C. 1 teaspoon (of cold cream)
   2 teaspoons (of cornstarch)
   1 teaspoon (of water)

Page 132
1, 2, 3
2, 1, 3
2, 3, 1
3, 2, 1

Page 133
1. They cleaned their rooms.
2. They washed the family's car.
3. They got ready to go to the zoo.
4. They visted the sharks.
5. They went to the wolf den.
6. They met their mother at the alligator exhibit.

Page 134
I woke up one morning feeling strange.
I got out of bed and looked in the mirror.
What a shock I got when I saw a plant growing out of my ears!
I ran to my mother to show her what had happened.
She said, "Those seeds you swallowed yesterday have planted inside you."
Then she looked in the phone book for a good gardener to come over to trim me.
I am feeling better now, but I still have to water myself every day.

Answer Key (cont.)

Page 135
1. Bake cookies for school on Tuesday.
2. Go to baseball practice on Wednesday.
3. Write my book report on Thursday.
4. Practice the violin on Friday.
5. Call Janet on Saturday.

Page 136
A. 2, 1, 5, 4, 3   E. 4, 2, 3, 1, 5
B. 1, 3, 5, 2, 4   F. 3, 5, 1, 2, 4
C. 4, 2, 1, 5, 3   G. 2, 1, 4, 3, 5
D. 3, 2, 4, 1, 5   H. 3, 5, 1, 2, 4

Page 137
1. football field   6. towels
2. bird   7. scissors
3. Beverly Hills   8. flowers
4. fortune cookies   9. tomato soup
5. diving board   10. spaghetti

Page 140
Julie and Juan want to work at the zoo.

Page 141
Answers will vary but should reflect these ideas:
1. Lola
2. loves to watch parrots
3. They are her favorite animals.
4. Lola loves to watch the parrots because they are her favorite animals.

Page 142
Answers will vary, but they should reflect the following ideas:
Mrs. Lee and her class are late for the bus.
The children enjoyed watching the penguins.

Page 143
1. It is about a very young boy named Max.
2. He watches baby penguins hatch.
3. He is nearby when they hatch.
4. Sentences will vary.
5. Pictures will vary.

Page 144
1. It is about George Washington.
2. He was a great leader.
3. He was a good general and president.
4. Sentences will vary.
5. Paragraphs will vary.

Page 145
1. She climbed down her bedpost.
2. She is glad her mother did not see the mess under her bed.
3. She arranges the dollhouse furniture.
4. They eat the girls' leftover cookies from her bedtime snack.
5. She actually finds cookie crumbs in her dollhouse.

Page 146
1. He was excited to pitch in the big game.
2. He had been practicing his pitching.
3. He rode his bicycle to the ballpark.
4. He warmed up in the bullpen.
5. He was named Most Valuable Player.

Page 147
Answers may vary but may include:
1. Karly says that the rain is a mess.
2. She can barely get through the flood.
3. She complains.

Page 148
1. Jack and Wendy do not like the Fun House.
2. They think it is too scary, and they want to leave.
1. Mary really wants the dress, and she is jealous.
2. Mary says that she does not like the dress, but she wants to know if there are any more. Also, by asking so much about it, she leads others to believe that she is really interested.

Page 149
1. *Alike:* eight years old, best friends, teaching each other their primary language, do homework together, popcorn is favorite snack, love Pete, enjoy the park, swing and slide with Pete
2. *Different:* Marta doesn't speak much English, Marta is from Mexico, Marta speaks Spanish well and Janis does not, Janis has a little brother and Marta has no siblings, Marta is a good skater, Janis has a scooter

Page 150
1. rooster   4. rose
2. movie   5. guitar
3. computer

Page 152–153
Answers will vary.

Page 154
1. F   6. O
2. O   7. O
3. O   8. F
4. F   9. F
5. F   10. O
1. Answers will vary.
2. Answers will vary.

Page 155
The following statements should be underlined (biased): 2, 4, 7, 8, and 9.

Page 156
1. excited   4. worried
2. sad   5. happy
3. funny

Page 157
Answers will vary.

Page 158
1. two
2. Tracy and his father
3. Tracy
4. "he" in first sentence

Page 159
1. check   4. check
2. no check   5. no check
3. check

Page 160
1. 3   3. 1
2. 1   4. 3

Page 161
1. Alicia   5. you and I
2. Luke and Chris   6. computer
3. movers   7. Tom; sisters
4. Sam

Page 162
1. It scared or shocked her.
2. His father got serious and set rules or limits.
3. She was ready to leave.
4. He had not felt well.
5. He slept soundly.
6. He was going to be in trouble.
7. "Stop."
8. "Are you scared, nervous, or changing your mind?"
9. He loves to tell a story.
10. She doesn't know what is happening.

Page 163
1. Dinner is free.
2. John was in a bad mood.
3. My cousin can grow plants very well.
4. When I have money, I have to spend it.
5. One should apologize for wrongdoings.
6. Cathy didn't know how things were done yet.
7. Mother told us to clean the house.
8. Dad gets up early.
9. The child wasn't out of danger.
10. Crystal was sad.

Page 164
Some answers may vary.
1. Los Angeles   11. pancakes
2. after noon   12. see
3. octagon   13. chicken
4. saw   14. Egypt
5. Texas   15. temperature
6. bed   16. 100
7. red   17. floor
8. cherries   18. pilot
9. Easter   19. hungry
10. mother   20. hive

Page 165
Some answers may vary.
1. smell   11. read
2. tennis   12. Braces
3. Elizabeth   13. right
4. poem   14. Swim
5. driver   15. ankle
6. Roosevelt   16. screwdriver
7. foot   17. fin
8. carpenter   18. fruit
9. den or cave   19. Oink
10. Frame   20. queen

Answer Key (cont.)

Page 166
1. little
2. foot
3. bee
4. floor
5. Car
6. girl
7. Door
8. eat
9. books
10. bottom
11. Green
12. waist
13. pilot
14. read
15. tree
16. eye
17. Night
18. December
19. cub
20. Nephew

Page 167
Some answers may vary.
1. holidays
2. girls' names
3. countries
4. fruits
5. farm animals
6. shades of purple
7. writing instruments
8. Disney characters
9. circus performers
10. colleges
11. rivers
12. directions
13. nursery rhymes
14. artists
15. former U.S. presidents
16. numbers
17. letters
18 baked goods
19. last names
20. tools

Page 168
animals: sloth, snipe, quetzal, meerkat, phoebe, peccary, toucan
fruits: strawberry, mango, quince, loganberry, papaya, guava, pineapple
flowers: primrose, gardenia, carnation, iris, crocus, impatiens, sweet William
sports: lacrosse, soccer, rugby, football, Ping-Pong, triathlon, kayaking
instruments: violin, bassoon, harp, trumpet, flute, mandolin, cello
clothing: moccasin, parka, poncho, trousers, tux, cummerbund, gown

Pages 169–180
Answers will vary.

Page 181
Answers will vary for the subjects or predicates added to each sentence.
1. S
2. S
3. P
4. S
5. P
6. S
7. P
8. P
9. P
10. S
11. S
12. P
13. S
14. P
15. S

Page 182
Answers will vary

Page 183
I love food, but I do not like to cook. First of all, I am not very good at cooking. I cut myself, I burn food, and I spill things that stain all my clothes. Then there is something about the ingredients that is a great mystery to me. I can follow a recipe very closely, but it never comes out right. The food might be too salty, too sweet, or just too weird. And then there's the mess. The food sticks to pots and pans and stains the sink. The floor, the dog, and I get covered in flour or onion juice. When I get finished with all that labor, I'm anxious to taste my masterpiece, but it is always a disappointment, and there are so many dishes that I don't have time to go out and get something really good to eat! I should just give up cooking altogether.

Page 184
1. tires, steering wheels, bumpers
2. refrigerators, ovens, frying pans
3. ears, knees, thumbs
4. lemons, dandelions, bananas

Pages 185–215
Writing will vary.

Page 216
1. 4
2. 13
3. 10
4. 12
5. 7
6. 6
7. 3
8. 8
9. 3
10. 10
11. 14
12. 8
13. 6
14. 11
15. 15
16. 5
17. 2
18. 8
19. 14
20. 7
21. 17
22. 13
23. 13
24. 14
25. 10
26. 9
27. 12
28. 10
29. 9
30. 9

Page 217
a. 108
b. 85
c. 55
d. 77
e. 76
f. 87
g. 148
h. 125
i. 42
j. 122

Page 218
a. 49 + 57 = $106
b. 26 + 32 = $58
c. 17 + 64 = $81
d. 32 + 57 = $89
e. 64 + 17 + 49 = $130
f. 26 + 57 + 32 = $115

Page 219
a. 83 + 24 + 16 = 123
b. 47 + 21 + 33 = 101
c. 14 + 32 + 24 = 70
d. 36 + 42 + 87 = 165

Page 220
a. 61
b. 106
c. 117
d. 37
e. 130
f. 81
g. 81
h. 110
i. 66
j. 63
k. 34
l. 93
m. 85
n. 130
o. 81
p. 137
q. 112
r. 183
s. 49
t. 109
u. 68
v. 110
w. 77
x. 130

Page 221
a. 143
b. 131
c. 91
d. 117
e. 186
f. 157
g. 123
h. 163
i. 145
j. 129
k. 185
l. 106
m. 156
n. 100
o. 93
p. 132
q. 201
r. 174
s. 150
t. 182
u. 174
v. 119
w. 111
x. 170

Page 222
1. 1599
2. 1233
3. 1852
4. 1408
5. 1316
6. 1402
7. 2157
8. 1871
9. 2174
10. 2061
11. 1074
12. 1767

Page 223
a. 14
b. 1
c. 7
d. 14
e. 30
f. 41
g. 26
h. 30
i. 60
j. 41

Page 224
a. 93 − 68 = 25
b. 43 − 40 = 3
c. 53 − 28 = 25
d. 83 − 62 = 21

Page 225
Across
1. fourteen
3. nineteen
7. seventeen
9. sixteen

Down
1. fifteen
2. twenty
4. eighteen
5. eleven
6. twelve
8. thirteen

Page 226
a. 1
b. 22
c. 71
d. 17
e. 26
f. 53
g. 57
h. 34
i. 30
j. 41
k. 4
l. 31
m. 53
n. 12
o. 55
p. 55
q. 52
r. 3
s. 23
t. 9
u. 34
v. 72
w. 15
x. 44

Answer Key (cont.)

Page 227

a.	8	i.	44	q.	4
b.	33	j.	40	r.	37
c.	31	k.	72	s.	32
d.	16	l.	21	t.	64
e.	62	m.	64	u.	59
f.	28	n.	31	v.	26
g.	47	o.	14	w.	5
h.	6	p.	15	x.	14

Page 228

1.	6	9.	9
2.	9	10.	7
3.	13	11.	23
4.	10	12.	11
5.	7	13.	8
6.	19	14.	6
7.	18	15.	24
8.	5	16.	12

Page 229

Possible Solutions:

1. $6 + 4 - 1 - 2 + 6 + 2 = 15$
2. $9 + 1 - 3 + 1 - 4 + 1 = 5$
3. $9 - 3 + 4 - 1 + 2 + 3 = 14$
4. $5 - 1 + 1 + 3 + 4 + 6 = 18$
5. $9 - 8 + 6 + 3 - 5 + 3 = 8$
6. $2 - 1 + 8 + 9 - 3 + 5 = 20$
7. $5 + 3 + 2 - 4 + 1 + 5 = 12$
8. $4 + 9 + 3 - 7 + 3 - 1 = 11$
9. $7 - 6 + 2 + 8 - 7 - 1 = 3$
10. $9 + 9 - 9 + 2 - 2 - 8 = 1$

Page 230

0 x 0 = 0	1 x 6 = 6	2 x 12 = 24	4 x 5 = 20
0 x 1 = 0	1 x 7 = 7	3 x 0 = 0	4 x 6 = 24
0 x 2 = 0	1 x 8 = 8	3 x 1 = 3	4 x 7 = 28
0 x 3 = 0	1 x 9 = 9	3 x 2 = 6	4 x 8 = 32
0 x 4 = 0	1 x 10 = 10	3 x 3 = 9	4 x 9 = 36
0 x 5 = 0	1 x 11 = 11	3 x 4 = 12	4 x 10 = 40
0 x 6 = 0	1 x 12 = 12	3 x 5 = 15	4 x 11 = 44
0 x 7 = 0	2 x 0 = 0	3 x 6 = 18	4 x 12 = 48
0 x 8 = 0	2 x 1 = 2	3 x 7 = 21	5 x 0 = 0
0 x 9 = 0	2 x 2 = 4	3 x 8 = 24	5 x 1 = 5
0 x 10 = 0	2 x 3 = 6	3 x 9 = 27	5 x 2 = 10
0 x 11 = 0	2 x 4 = 8	3 x 10 = 30	5 x 3 = 15
0 x 12 = 0	2 x 5 = 10	3 x 11 = 33	5 x 4 = 20
1 x 0 = 0	2 x 6 = 12	3 x 12 = 36	5 x 5 = 25
1 x 1 = 1	2 x 7 = 14	4 x 0 = 0	5 x 6 = 30
1 x 2 = 2	2 x 8 = 16	4 x 1 = 4	5 x 7 = 35
1 x 3 = 3	2 x 9 = 18	4 x 2 = 8	5 x 8 = 40
1 x 4 = 4	2 x 10 = 20	4 x 3 = 12	5 x 9 = 45
1 x 5 = 5	2 x 11 = 22	4 x 4 = 16	5 x 10 = 50

Page 231

5 x 11 = 55	7 x 4 = 28	8 x 10 = 80	10 x 3 = 30	11 x 9 = 99
5 x 12 = 60	7 x 5 = 35	8 x 11 = 88	10 x 4 = 40	11 x 10 = 110
6 x 0 = 0	7 x 6 = 42	8 x 12 = 96	10 x 5 = 50	11 x 11 = 121
6 x 1 = 6	7 x 7 = 49	9 x 0 = 0	10 x 6 = 60	11 x 12 = 132
6 x 2 = 12	7 x 8 = 56	9 x 1 = 9	10 x 7 = 70	12 x 0 = 0
6 x 3 = 18	7 x 9 = 63	9 x 2 = 18	10 x 8 = 80	12 x 1 = 12
6 x 4 = 24	7 x 10 = 70	9 x 3 = 27	10 x 9 = 90	12 x 2 = 24
6 x 5 = 30	7 x 11 = 77	9 x 4 = 36	10 x 10 = 100	12 x 3 = 36
6 x 6 = 36	7 x 12 = 84	9 x 5 = 45	10 x 11 = 110	12 x 4 = 48
6 x 7 = 42	8 x 0 = 0	9 x 6 = 54	10 x 12 = 120	12 x 5 = 60
6 x 8 = 48	8 x 1 = 8	9 x 7 = 63	11 x 0 = 0	12 x 6 = 72
6 x 9 = 54	8 x 2 = 16	9 x 8 = 72	11 x 1 = 11	12 x 7 = 84
6 x 10 = 60	8 x 3 = 24	9 x 9 = 81	11 x 2 = 22	12 x 8 = 96
6 x 11 = 66	8 x 4 = 32	9 x 10 = 90	11 x 3 = 33	12 x 9 = 108
6 x 12 = 72	8 x 5 = 40	9 x 11 = 99	11 x 4 = 44	12 x 10 = 120
7 x 0 = 0	8 x 6 = 48	9 x 12 = 108	11 x 5 = 55	12 x 11 = 132
7 x 1 = 7	8 x 7 = 56	10 x 0 = 0	11 x 6 = 66	12 x 12 = 144
7 x 2 = 14	8 x 8 = 64	10 x 1 = 10	11 x 7 = 77	
7 x 3 = 21	8 x 9 = 72	10 x 2 = 20	11 x 8 = 88	

Page 232

2 x 2 = 4	12 x 5 = 60	6 x 1 = 6	6 x 3 = 18
3 x 8 = 24	7 x 5 = 35	7 x 7 = 49	7 x 9 = 63
5 x 1 = 5	11 x 8 = 88	9 x 0 = 0	9 x 2 = 18
10 x 0 = 0	10 x 4 = 40	10 x 6 = 60	10 x 8 = 80
2 x 3 = 6	11 x 10 = 110	11 x 12 = 132	12 x 1 = 12
11 x 5 = 55	6 x 0 = 0	6 x 2 = 12	6 x 4 = 24
7 x 4 = 28	7 x 6 = 42	7 x 8 = 56	10 x 7 = 70
10 x 8 = 80	12 x 8 = 96	9 x 1 = 9	9 x 3 = 27
10 x 3 = 30	10 x 5 = 50	10 x 7 = 70	10 x 9 = 90
11 x 9 = 99	11 x 11 = 121	12 x 0 = 0	12 x 2 = 24

Page 233

96 x 16 = 1,536	68 x 88 = 5,984	56 x 75 = 4,200	22 x 67 = 1,474
90 x 13 = 1,170	33 x 31 = 1,023	84 x 28 = 2,352	74 x 17 = 1,258
47 x 19 = 893	20 x 62 = 1,240	70 x 96 = 6,720	26 x 93 = 2,418
25 x 11 = 275	24 x 19 = 456	58 x 75 = 4,350	14 x 72 = 1,008
26 x 16 = 416	41 x 40 = 1,640	50 x 10 = 500	48 x 30 = 1,440
40 x 28 = 1,120	46 x 20 = 920	21 x 25 = 525	42 x 48 = 2,016
82 x 35 = 2,870	49 x 71 = 3,479	77 x 63 = 4,851	88 x 50 = 4,400
60 x 52 = 3,120	38 x 45 = 1,710	79 x 44 = 3,476	69 x 18 = 1,242
71 x 27 = 1,917	24 x 35 = 840	86 x 33 = 2,838	43 x 31 = 1,333
32 x 54 = 1,728	27 x 32 = 864	13 x 29 = 377	19 x 22 = 418

Page 234

173 x 6 = 1,038	533 x 8 = 4,264	138 x 2 = 276	833 x 5 = 4,165
227 x 3 = 681	388 x 1 = 388	417 x 8 = 3,336	524 x 3 = 1,572
402 x 1 = 402	620 x 6 = 3,720	317 x 4 = 1,268	468 x 6 = 2,808
420 x 8 = 3,360	662 x 3 = 1,986	458 x 7 = 3,206	947 x 2 = 1,894
178 x 9 = 1,602	714 x 9 = 6,426	550 x 6 = 3,300	767 x 7 = 5,369
324 x 8 = 2,592	835 x 3 = 2,505	594 x 5 = 2,970	632 x 3 = 1,896
172 x 4 = 688	152 x 7 = 1,064	180 x 4 = 720	221 x 2 = 442
286 x 8 = 2,288	254 x 5 = 1,270	538 x 1 = 538	489 x 4 = 1,956
509 x 4 = 2,036	851 x 1 = 851	728 x 6 = 4,368	141 x 9 = 1,269
615 x 2 = 1,230	674 x 8 = 5,392	107 x 3 = 321	213 x 5 = 1,065

Page 235

23 x 16 = 368	13 x 38 = 494	89 x 57 = 5,073	44 x 76 = 3,344
90 x 39 = 3,510	31 x 11 = 341	24 x 23 = 552	22 x 51 = 1,122
17 x 79 = 1,343	41 x 96 = 3,936	74 x 19 = 1,406	16 x 39 = 624
35 x 15 = 525	14 x 79 = 1,106	48 x 79 = 3,792	25 x 17 = 425
14 x 63 = 882	80 x 54 = 4,320	70 x 71 = 4,970	28 x 93 = 2,604
56 x 82 = 4,592	34 x 24 = 816	21 x 26 = 546	58 x 48 = 2,784
73 x 50 = 3,650	46 x 27 = 1,242	67 x 64 = 4,288	99 x 56 = 5,544
50 x 28 = 1,400	68 x 40 = 2,720	39 x 42 = 1,638	64 x 48 = 3,072
81 x 76 = 6,156	34 x 83 = 2,822	96 x 30 = 2,880	34 x 23 = 782
51 x 44 = 2,244	23 x 36 = 828	18 x 28 = 504	36 x 20 = 720

Page 236

0 ÷ 0 = 0	6 ÷ 1 = 6	24 ÷ 12 = 2	24 ÷ 4 = 6
1 ÷ 0 = 0	7 ÷ 1 = 7	3 ÷ 3 = 1	28 ÷ 4 = 7
2 ÷ 0 = 0	8 ÷ 1 = 8	6 ÷ 3 = 2	32 ÷ 4 = 8
3 ÷ 0 = 0	9 ÷ 1 = 9	9 ÷ 3 = 3	36 ÷ 4 = 9
4 ÷ 0 = 0	10 ÷ 1 = 10	12 ÷ 3 = 4	40 ÷ 4 = 10
6 ÷ 0 = 0	11 ÷ 1 = 11	15 ÷ 3 = 5	44 ÷ 4 = 11
7 ÷ 0 = 0	12 ÷ 1 = 12	18 ÷ 3 = 6	48 ÷ 4 = 12
8 ÷ 0 = 0	2 ÷ 2 = 1	21 ÷ 3 = 7	5 ÷ 5 = 1
9 ÷ 0 = 0	4 ÷ 2 = 2	24 ÷ 3 = 8	10 ÷ 5 = 2
10 ÷ 0 = 0	6 ÷ 2 = 3	27 ÷ 3 = 9	15 ÷ 5 = 3
11 ÷ 0 = 0	8 ÷ 2 = 4	30 ÷ 3 = 10	20 ÷ 5 = 4
12 ÷ 0 = 0	10 ÷ 2 = 5	33 ÷ 3 = 11	25 ÷ 5 = 5
1 ÷ 0 = 0	12 ÷ 2 = 6	36 ÷ 3 = 12	30 ÷ 5 = 6
1 ÷ 1 = 1	14 ÷ 2 = 7	4 ÷ 4 = 1	35 ÷ 5 = 7
2 ÷ 1 = 2	16 ÷ 2 = 8	8 ÷ 4 = 2	40 ÷ 5 = 8
3 ÷ 1 = 3	18 ÷ 2 = 9	12 ÷ 4 = 3	45 ÷ 5 = 9
4 ÷ 1 = 4	20 ÷ 2 = 10	16 ÷ 4 = 4	50 ÷ 5 = 10
5 ÷ 1 = 5	22 ÷ 2 = 11	20 ÷ 4 = 5	55 ÷ 5 = 11

Answer Key (cont.)

Page 237

60 ÷ 5 = 12	42 ÷ 7 = 6	96 ÷ 8 = 12	60 ÷ 10 = 6	132 ÷ 11 = 12
6 ÷ 6 = 1	49 ÷ 7 = 7	9 ÷ 9 = 1	70 ÷ 10 = 7	12 ÷ 12 = 1
12 ÷ 6 = 2	56 ÷ 7 = 8	18 ÷ 9 = 2	80 ÷ 10 = 8	24 ÷ 12 = 2
18 ÷ 6 = 3	63 ÷ 7 = 9	27 ÷ 9 = 3	90 ÷ 10 = 9	36 ÷ 12 = 3
24 ÷ 6 = 4	70 ÷ 7 = 10	36 ÷ 9 = 4	100 ÷ 10 = 10	48 ÷ 12 = 4
30 ÷ 6 = 5	77 ÷ 7 = 11	45 ÷ 9 = 5	110 ÷ 10 = 11	60 ÷ 12 = 5
36 ÷ 6 = 6	84 ÷ 7 = 12	54 ÷ 9 = 6	120 ÷ 10 = 12	72 ÷ 12 = 6
42 ÷ 6 = 7	8 ÷ 8 = 1	63 ÷ 9 = 7	11 ÷ 11 = 1	84 ÷ 12 = 7
48 ÷ 6 = 8	16 ÷ 8 = 2	72 ÷ 9 = 8	22 ÷ 11 = 2	96 ÷ 12 = 8
54 ÷ 6 = 9	24 ÷ 8 = 3	81 ÷ 9 = 9	33 ÷ 11 = 3	108 ÷ 12 = 9
60 ÷ 6 = 10	32 ÷ 8 = 4	90 ÷ 9 = 10	44 ÷ 11 = 4	120 ÷ 12 = 10
66 ÷ 6 = 11	40 ÷ 8 = 5	99 ÷ 9 = 11	55 ÷ 11 = 5	132 ÷ 12 = 11
72 ÷ 6 = 12	48 ÷ 8 = 6	108 ÷ 9 = 12	66 ÷ 11 = 6	144 ÷ 12 = 12
7 ÷ 7 = 1	56 ÷ 8 = 7	10 ÷ 10 = 1	77 ÷ 11 = 7	
14 ÷ 7 = 2	64 ÷ 8 = 8	20 ÷ 10 = 2	88 ÷ 11 = 8	
21 ÷ 7 = 3	72 ÷ 8 = 9	30 ÷ 10 = 3	99 ÷ 11 = 9	
28 ÷ 7 = 4	80 ÷ 8 = 10	40 ÷ 10 = 4	110 ÷ 11 = 10	
35 ÷ 7 = 5	88 ÷ 8 = 11	50 ÷ 10 = 5	121 ÷ 11 = 11	

Page 238

400 ÷ 16 = 25
225 ÷ 15 = 15
234 ÷ 18 = 13
240 ÷ 12 = 20
180 ÷ 10 = 18
136 ÷ 8 = 17
95 ÷ 5 = 19
248 ÷ 8 = 31
112 ÷ 2 = 56
256 ÷ 16 = 16
150 ÷ 6 = 25
128 ÷ 32 = 4
288 ÷ 16 = 18
171 ÷ 9 = 19
231 ÷ 11 = 21

Page 239

1. 5 + 7 = 12
2. 24 ÷ 4 = 6
3. 9 + 3 = 12
4. 18 − 6 = 12
5. 4 + 9 = 13
6. 4 x 9 = 36
7. 10 x 8 = 80
8. 15 ÷ 5 = 3
9. 11 ÷ 4 = 7
10. 8 + 16 = 24
11. 2 x 8 = 16
12. 3 + 2 = 5
13. 22 − 6 = 16
14. 9 + 1 = 10
15. 3 x 3 = 9
16. 144 ÷ 12 = 12
17. 21 ÷ 3 = 7
18. 90 ÷ 10 = 9
19. 12 x 11 = 132
20. 14 x 1 = 14

Page 240

1. 1/3
2. 1/4
3. 5/8
4. 3/5
5. 7/10
6. 2/6 = 1/3
7. 3/4
8. 1/2

Page 241

Page 242

1. watermelon
2. grapes
3. 1) watermelon, 2) peaches, 3) plums, 4) apricots, 5) grapes
4. 1/2; 1/4; 1/8
5. Answers will vary.

Page 243

1. 30 minutes; five minutes; five minutes; 10 minutes; 10 minutes
2. Answers will vary.

Graphs will vary.

Page 244

Answers are approximate measurements.

1. 4 meters
2. 9 meters
3. 12.5 meters
4. 13 meters
5. 15.5 meters

Page 245

Answers will vary but may include:

1. a
2. f
3. c, e
4. b, d
5. d
6. d
7. b, d
8. f
9. c, e
10. a

Page 246

Answers are approximate measurements.

1. 18 miles
2. 10 miles
3. 35 miles
4. 18 miles
5. 16 miles
6. 10 miles

It is farther from Pleasantown to Mountaintown.

Answer Key (cont.)

Page 247
1. 1,750
2. 550
3. 450
4. 1,150
5. 1,400
6. 1,050
7. 850
8. 600
9. 600
10. 600

Page 248
1. one cent
2. five cents
3. ten cents
4. Answers will vary, but the first number should always be divided by five to get the second number.
5. Answers will vary, but the first number should always be divided by two to get the second number.
6. Answers will vary, but the first number should always be divided by ten to get the second number.
7. one nickel
8. one dime
9. one dime
10. 16 cents

Page 249
1. 1 silver dollar
2. 3 q, 2 d, 1 n
3. 2 q, 5 d
4. 10 d
5. 5 d, 10 n
6. 2 q, 4 d, 10 p
7. 7 d, 5 n, 5 p
8. 9 d, 10 p
9. 1 q, 3 d, 6 n, 15 p
10. 3 q, 25 p

Page 250
Answers will vary. Accept all that add to fifty cents.

Page 251
Answers will vary. Accept all that add to one dollar.

Page 252
1. P.M.
2. A.M.
3. P.M.
4. P.M.
5. A.M.
6. A.M.
7. P.M.
8. P.M.
9. P.M.
10. A.M.
11. A.M.
12. P.M.
13. P.M.
14. A.M.
15. P.M.
16. P.M.
17. A.M.
18. P.M.
19. P.M.
20. A.M.

Page 253
1. *second*: one-sixtieth of a minute
2. *minute*: 60 seconds
3. *hour*: 60 minutes
4. *day*: 24 hours
5. *week*: seven days
6. *fortnight*: two weeks
7. *month*: approximately four weeks (28–31 days)
8. *year*: 365 days
9. *decade*: 10 years
10. *score*: 20 years
11. *century*: 100 years
12. *millennium*: 1,000 years

Page 254
Lucy = B
Gwen = C-
Cara = A
Martin = C
Donald = D

Page 255
Ted Agee, 9
Theodore Chin, 8
Teddy Dalton, 10

Page 256
Chad = Reds
Danny = Cardinals
Andrew = White Sox
Ryan = Dodgers
Will = A's

Page 257
Katelyn—roller coaster, bratwurst
Kenny—Ferris wheel, hot dogs
Emily—bumper cars, hamburger
Howie—carousel, corndog

Page 258
Jane = 5
Daisy = 2
Carrie = 9
Joanne = 3
Gertie = 4
Annie = 6
Penny = 8
Tammy = 1
Lindsey = 7

Page 259
1. southeast
2. west
3. northeast
4. southwest
5. south
6. north
7. east
8. northwest

Page 260
Home = last row fourth house from the left

Answer Key (cont.)

Page 261
1. true
2. false; western and southeastern
3. false; northeast
4. false; only one, the others are reached by local roads
5. true
6. true
7. false; west of lake, east of railroad
8. true

Page 262
example: silver
A1, white; D3, gray; B4, red; D2, ivory
C4, silver; A2, yellow; D1, black; C2, purple
B3, tan; A4, gold; C3, brown; B1, pink
D4, lavender; B2, green; A3, orange; C1, blue
shaded: A1, A3, B3, C2
striped: B2, C1, C3
unmarked: A2, B1

Page 263
1. E2
2. F3
3. C1, D1, E1
4. E5
5. E3
6. A3, A4, B3, B4
7. F1, F2
8. A5, A6
9. D5
10. C4
11. E6
12. B1
13. D4
14. B5
15. C6
16. C2

Page 264
1. Southern, Eastern
2. Northern, Eastern
3. Northern, Western
4. Northern, Western
5. Northern, Eastern
6. Northern, Western
7. Northern, Eastern
8. Northern, Eastern
9. Northern, Western
10. Southern, Western
11. Northern, Eastern
12. Northern, Western
13. Northern, Eastern
14. Southern, Western
15. Southern, Eastern
16. Southern, Eastern

Page 265
1. Grand Junction
2. Sterling
3. Denver
4. Lamar
5. Durango
6. Colorado Springs
7. Glenwood Springs
8. Campo
9. Craig
10. Kanorado

Page 266
1. 35 and 40
2. 27
3. Wayne
4. Glen Ridge, 33
5. a. 15
   b. 37
   c. 27
   d. 48

Page 267
1. a. 31
   b. 45
   c. 37
   d. 88
   e. 51
   f. 85
2. a. 6
   b. 14
   c. 29
   d. 45
   e. 66
   f. 29
3. a. 99
   b. 62
   c. 66
   d. 59
   e. 45
   f. 71

Page 268
1. east
2. Ekalaka
3. Boyes, Hammond, Alzada
4. Boxelder Creek
5. Medicine Rocks

Page 269
1. Far North
2. Southwestern
3. Pacific Coast
4. Plains

Page 270
1. Brunswick
2. fruit
3. pecans, peanuts, tobacco (Other choices are possible.)
4. berries
5. corn
6. marble, granite

Page 271
1. Sacramento, Oakland, San Francisco, San Jose, Los Angeles, San Diego
2. Needles, Barstow
3. 75 to 100
4. Crescent City, Redding, Bakersfield
5. Answers will vary. Accept logically explained answers, such as desert conditions in Needles and Barstow.

Page 272
1. Boston
2. Plymouth, New Bedford
3. Boston: Below 22 F, Below -6 C
   Lowell: 22 to 26 F, -6 to -3 C
   Pittsfield: 26 to 30 F, -3 to -1 C

Page 273
1. D3, A1, C3
2. A1, D1
3. State Highway 106
4. B1, B2, C1, C2
5. Mount McGee, Remington, Carlton
6. 16, 22
7. coastline

Page 274
Answers are in miles.
1. 2786
2. 1440
3. 206
4. 2037
5. 802
6. 840
7. 1329
8. 1058
9. 2873
10. 2976
11. 963
12. 417

Page 275
1. obsidian
2. sedimentary
3. metamorphic

Page 276
1. David Peterson
2. $5.80—Kathryn Ross
3. Barbara Marshall
4. no
5. no
6. 614
7. $48.00

Page 277
1. Halloween party
2. Spring Celebration
3. Valentine's Day party
4. 4

Page 278
Time lines will vary.

Page 279
1. 5 pianos, 10 flutes, 30 guitars, 15 drums, 5 trumpets
2. 25, 20, 15, 25
3. Accept any reasonable response.

Page 280
1. acoustic and electric guitar
2. tuning keys, fingerboard, frets, and bridge
3. soundboard and sound hole
4. pickups, base, treble, and volume controls

Page 282
#1 = M, #2 = W, #3 = V

Answer Key (cont.)

Page 283
1. no
2. 5:00 P.M.
3. no
4. *A Lad*, *Dan*, and *The Mystery Garden*
5. *The Sandy Lot* and *The Mystery Garden*
6. Answers will vary.

Page 284
Alaska, Hawaii, Oregon, Nevada, Montana, South Dakota, Oklahoma, Arkansas, Illinois, Kentucky, Georgia, West Virginia, New York, Vermont, New Hampshire, Maine

Page 285
Finland, Germany, England, Venezuela, Peru, Mexico, New Zealand, Australia, Mongolia, India, Pakistan, Saudi Arabia, Egypt, Chad, Italy, France, Ireland, Iceland, Canada

Page 286
Los Angeles—United States
Glasgow—Scotland
Seoul—South Korea
Bombay—India
Nagano—Japan
Nice—France
Frankfurt—Germany
Florence—Italy
Toronto—Canada
Lima—Peru
Rio de Janeiro—Brazil
Bogota—Colombia
Lisbon—Portugal
Cairo—Egypt
Jerusalem—Israel
Copenhagen—Denmark
Canberra—Australia
Dublin—Ireland
Cape Town—South Africa
Acapulco—Mexico

Page 287
Alabama

Page 288
Utah

Page 289
Argentina

Page 290
Nigeria